ENDORSEMENTS

"It was the end-1990's when I first met Dr. Forrest Weiland. He arrived to Zaporozhzhia to teach at Zaporizhzhia Bible Seminary which was established in 1994 and continues to train Christian workers today. Dr. Weiland faithfully supported ministry of ZBS in Ukraine for many years. His book *The Vindication of Messiah on Earth* is the result of Dr. Weiland's many years of ministry as a Bible teacher in theological schools and churches. In his book, he explains that *the writers of Scripture focus on the major stages and progressive unfolding of God's purpose of recovering mankind from the fall, regaining the earth, and establishing Messiah's rule over it. ... History is moving inexorably toward this goal: Messiah will be vindicated, the Son shall reign on the earth.* All of this must happen during the millennium kingdom. Messiah must reign on the earth!

I highly commend this theological work to you."

VOLODYMYR DEGTYARYOV
Former President, Zaporizhzhia Bible Seminary, Ukraine

"Forrest Weiland's *Vindication of Messiah on Earth* is a breath of fresh air for any scholar, pastor or Bible student looking for a balanced view of the Messiah and His millennial kingdom. He masterfully places in historical and theological context the purpose and nature of God's kingdom through an analysis of Israel's history, captivity, and covenants. The description of the millennial period is worth its weight in gold as he answers the tough questions regarding the temple, sacrifices, and worship. The book not only feeds the reader's mind, but also nourishes the soul!"

JOSEPH M. HOLDEN
President, Veritas International University

"It is a distinct privilege to recommend, with my highest praise, the work by Forrest Weiland entitled *The Vindication of Messiah on Earth* for its close exegetical analysis of the largest number of texts on this subject seen in most works that are written on this subject. Readers will find one of the most extensive discussions of the key subjects on the Bible's treatment of the Last Days of earth's history and the Coming of our Lord Jesus Christ in that future day. There could not be a more appropriate topic in this critical period of time in our lives. This is a volume that should be widely read and discussed."

Cordially,

WALTER C. KAISER, JR.
President Emeritus, Gordon-Conwell Theological Seminary

"*The Vindication of the Messiah on Earth* by Dr. Forrest Weiland, is the most significant book on the establishment of God's kingdom on earth that I have read in the past fifty years. The book enables the reader not only to understand the purpose of the Bible, but to place what may be perplexing portions of the Bible in their proper context. The books of the Bible will no longer be seen as a compilation of historical events, but significant milestones on a road map leading the reader closer and closer to the climax and purpose of human history."

FRED W. MCRAE
Missionary Global Outreach International

"At this crucial moment in human history when so many are troubled and looking everywhere for solutions to the problems and divisions humanity faces, Dr. Forrest Weiland's timely book *The Vindication of the Messiah on Earth* reminds of where our hope is to be placed, in the return and the reign of King Jesus! It is only when see and embrace the overarching biblical narrative of a Messiah that will not only redeem but will reign that we find comfort for our souls in the midst of the chaotic world we live in. I highly recommend this work!"

DAVID FANDEY
Lead Pastor of The Fields

THE

VINDICATION

OF

MESSIAH

ON EARTH

Tracing Jesus and His Kingdom
from Genesis to Revelation

FORREST S. WEILAND

LAMPION
House Publishing

LAMPION HOUSE PUBLISHING, LLC
Navasota, Texas 77868
2023

The Vindication of Messiah on Earth

Lampion House Publishing, LLC
P.O. Box 1295
Navasota, TX 77868
Website: http://lampionhousepublishing.com/

ISBN: 979-8-9878598-6-5 (softcover)

Cover design by Ben Weiland
Interior Design/Formatting by Vickie Swisher, Studio 20|20

Printed in the United States of America

To Sue, my wife and best friend,
who worked long and hard in her own profession,
allowing me time for study, teaching, and writing this book,
and to my son Ben and his wife Marisa
with whom I love to talk Bible and Theology.

CONTENTS

CHAPTER 3
IDENTIFYING THE RIGHTFUL RULER   27

CHAPTER 4
NEW TESTAMENT KINGDOM DEVELOPMENTS   31

CHAPTER 5
MYSTERIES OF THE KINGDOM   45

CHAPTER 6
FREQUENT OBJECTIONS TO THE MILLENNIUM   55

FOREWORD

H. WAYNE HOUSE, TH.D., J.D.

*Distinguished Research Professor
of Theology, Law, and Culture
at Faith International University*

Over the last few decades, several books have been published that deal with the subject of the last days, the premillennial coming of Christ, and his future kingdom on the earth. There are few, however, who set forth their evidence from Scripture as thoroughly or as well as Forrest Weiland in his new book *The Vindication of Messiah on Earth*.

Dr. Weiland starts off his book by setting forth the nature of interpretation, since many prophetic utterances in the Bible have wrongly been interpreted allegorically rather than literally. The Reformation did well in wrenching the church from the excesses of allegorical interpretation that came from Alexandria, through Jerome, Augustine, and others during the medieval period. Unfortunately, with regards to prophecy, many of the Reformers continued to embrace an allegorical method of interpretation as do many contemporary interpreters.

Having edited a book on Biblical Hermeneutics with Dr. Weiland, I can attest to his understanding of the science of biblical interpretation. He has examined the important Old Testament prophetic passages that concern the coming of Messiah and the nature of His kingdom. In *Vindication of Messiah on Earth* the author has interpreted each passage of Scripture in a clear and organized manner so that the average reader can understand the development of God plan for his Messiah and his kingdom.

Dr. Weiland has written a balanced view that is a clear and concise presentation of the biblical teaching of God's plan for the earth that will be accomplished through the work of His Anointed One, Jesus. Difficult questions that are often on the mind of the biblical reader will likely be addressed and clarified. The reader will find it helpful to have such a concise work regarding God's plans for His people Israel and the church that gives careful and proper treatment of the various arguments relating to the Messiah's future rule on the earth.

INTRODUCTION

WHAT'S THE BIBLE ALL ABOUT?

The Bible is arguably the most read book in the world today and in human history. According to Guinness World Records, it is the best-selling book of all time with over five billion copies sold and distributed worldwide. What makes this book so popular? What is it all about? It is a question that Bible students, scholars, and casual readers alike ask. Depending on who you ask, the answer varies. The answer is not only of interest to the evangelical community, but also to non-church goers, and even atheists who wonder why this book has generated such attention over the centuries. What is the general overall subject of the Bible? This is a question I would like to try and address in this book.

To answer this question about the overall subject of the Bible, we have to dive into history, because the Scripture covers so many historical periods. We will also need to wrestle with theology because the Bible is ultimately a book about God and his purposes with the world and beyond. To a lesser degree we will need to consider a few literary genres in the Bible because those genres inform our interpretation. Ultimately, we will need to apply hermeneutics (theory of interpretation) to this task. But in all this, I do not want us to—so to speak—"miss the forest for the trees." My goal is for the reader to acquire a general understanding of what the Bible is all about.

INTERPRETATION: LANGUAGE MATTERS

Of course, understanding often comes down to the question of hermeneutics. How we interpret the Scripture will determine to a large degree what we think the Scripture is teaching. Although this book is not a treatise on hermeneutics, in my interpretation of biblical texts, particularly prophetic texts, I will simply attempt to take the words that the biblical writers use in their particular historical contexts in their normal sense. This does not mean the writers never use figurative or poetic language, but it does mean we honor the writers by letting their texts—in their contexts—say what they say. Only by this method can we arrive at the author's intended or actual meaning, rather than imposing our own preferred meaning upon the text. In all this, I will be the first to admit, I can be wrong in my interpretations, but I will always be honest with what the Scripture is saying.

Only through this approach can we dispel the skeptics who charge that every interpretation is merely a matter of personal bias. They conclude that Scripture means whatever the interpreter happens to fancy. Such a conclusion empties the Word (and any text) of its intended meaning, purpose, and power. This subjective approach is unfair to the human writers and unfair to the divine Author. So, I would argue that interpretation is not a matter of personal preference. Rather, we must allow the Bible to say what it says through observing its genre, grammar, and historical context so that we might correctly deduce what the author intended to say and mean. In this way, we can gain confidence and assurance regarding what the Bible purports. Otherwise, we would be left with merely a menagerie of human opinions about the Bible. Happily, the biblical writers have given us examples of how they have interpreted other biblical writers. Through their example of interpreting biblical texts, we see that the words of Scripture were intended to be understood in their normal semantic sense.

My desire in this book is not to be polemical, but I realize some or even many may disagree with what I am purporting.

That would probably be the case no matter what position I take in interpreting the Bible. Nevertheless, I feel it is a worthy task to focus on this question, what is the Bible all about?

THE BIBLE: AN UNFOLDING REVELATION OF GOD'S PURPOSE FOR MANKIND

Though the Bible was written over a 1500-year period of time and consists of sixty-six books, it is nevertheless a unity, one book, one coherent story, an epic drama. Though there were more than forty contributing writers, there was just one mind that directed them all. I Timothy 3:16 begins, "All Scripture is inspired by God." So, we consider the Bible not merely as a collection of six-ty-six loosely related books, but rather as a divine revelation produced by one mind and thus without any internal contradiction.

This point is made numerous times and in numerous ways throughout the Word of God. In Psalm 19:7 David states, "The law of the Lord is perfect." Proverbs 30:5 says, "every word of God is tested," and Psalm 12:6 emphasizes that "the words of the Lord are pure words; as silver tried in a furnace on the earth, refined seven times." Since the Word was given by one divine mind, we can expect that this revelation will perfectly harmonize with itself. Since each human author is "moved" by the one divine author (2 Pet 1:21), they are not at odds with each other in their teaching, even though they may be separated by centuries and cultures. It is true that each book has its unique and unified message, but there is also a sense in which the individual books combine to make a whole that is the sum of the individual parts.

THE UNITY OF THE BIBLE AND ITS MESSAGE

Saint Jerome was purported to have said, "The Scriptures are shallow enough for a babe to come and drink without fear of drowning and deep enough for theologians to swim in without ever touching the bottom."[1] By that he meant that the Bible is so simple that even children can understand it and yet so profound that the erudite scholar must admit that he is unable to plumb its depths. The major truths of the Scriptures are readily discerned. This is often referred to as the perspicuity or clarity of the Bible. It was written to be understood.[2] However, it is also true that some passages are more difficult than others to interpret or understand.

The fact that God's word is a revelation points to the reality that God did not intend for the Scriptures to be a mystery, but rather He intended for them to be understood. How could God expect obedience to any of his commands if his words were not clear and ascertainable? This does not mean that all of the Scripture is equally clear, but it does mean all of it is generally accessible to our understanding.

Even though there are many passages in the Bible that challenge our understanding, most of our attempts to find a plausible interpretation derive from the belief that God's word comes from One mind that does not contradict itself. God's thinking is not at odds with itself. When we consider that it was written by over forty authors over a period of 1500 hundred years employing three languages and on three continents, its consistency is nothing short of a miracle.

When we assert that God inspired the Scriptures, we mean they were "God-breathed;" not that God dictated them (though there are parts dictated by God), but that God the Holy Spirit oversaw or superintended each of the authors so that they wrote

---

1   Since the Apostle Paul teaches that "natural man," the man without God's Spirit, cannot understand the things of God, we can assume that Jerome is referring to the child or theologian who comes to the Scriptures with an open and believing heart (1 Cor 2:10-14).

2   When God created man in his image, He did so giving him the capacity to acquire and employ language (Gen 1:26; 2:19-20). For example, the first task given to Adam was the verbal task of naming the animals (Gen 2:19-20). History demonstrates that this verbal language capacity ostensibly includes not only the acquired ability to speak but also the learned ability to write. Admittedly, not every person or people group is literate, but apart from certain physical or mental limitations the capacity for literacy appears to be innate in man. Where widespread illiteracy is prevalent, factors such as opportunity and education rather than capacity present the limitation. The point is that the Scriptures belong to the medium of human language and thus their meaning is accessible.

using their own personality, skill, and acumen to communicate in various written forms what God wanted to say. This does not refer to some personal artistic inspiration that the writers possessed, but rather to the process of writing the Bible in its various genres by many different authors. God the Spirit miraculously worked in a multiplicity of ways to move each author to write his portion of Scripture (Heb 1:1; 2 Pet 1:21). This is why the authors, though in some cases separated by centuries, cultures, and languages, nevertheless, do not contradict one another. The unity arises from the one mind that was the source of all that was written, the mind of God.

The Bible itself testifies regarding God that it is impossible for Him to lie (Num 23:19; Tit 1:2; Heb 6:18). So, there is no confusion or essential disagreement between Moses and Jesus, or Paul and James, etc. All that they wrote was from one divine source and harmonizes perfectly. This would lead us to assert that there may well be paradoxes in the Bible but not contradictions. This also considers that different theological content was directed towards specific audiences for specific times. For example, in the Mosaic Law just because the faithful Jewish believer was to bring an animal for an offering, this does not mean that a faithful believer in the church today must also do the same. One writer may emphasize the responsibilities of the believer living in a particular age, while another writer may speak to believers living in a different time and under a different arrangement of God's rule. These are differences, but these are not contradictions. This unity of truth leads us to expect that there is a continuity in the Bible's message. It is an unfolding drama beginning at creation in Genesis 1–2 and ending with the new heaven and earth in Revelation 21–22.

Though the mind of God is without contradiction, unfortunately the same cannot be said of us who interpret the Bible. Interpreters of the Scripture think very differently when it comes to theology and what we think or claim the Bible is all about.

Even though we know that we must depend upon the Spirit of God in the interpretive process, unlike the writers of Scripture, we are fallible, very fallible. The best we can do is to validate our interpretations though the information given in the text and its context. The information in the text itself must lead us to what appears to be the most plausible interpretation. When all is said and done, experience has shown us that even godly scholars will differ. It's at this point a well-known quotation (by a reputably unknown source) is helpful. The quote states, "In essentials unity, in non-essentials liberty, and in all things charity."

Some doctrines are essential for every believer to hold to, other doctrines fall into a category of less importance, and there we grant grace to one another and liberty to our brothers and sisters who differ from us in their understanding of God's word. But in all things, we need to be charitable towards one another even when we disagree over important doctrines.

FINDING THE FOCAL POINT OF THE SCRIPTURES

Many answers can be proffered when we pose the questions: what is the Bible about, what is the major message? Let's briefly consider a couple oft-proposed subjects by asking a few questions.

Is the Bible a book about man?

The answer here is, of course, yes. Much is said about man: his origin, his fall, his character, his value to God, etc. Yet, much is not said. Most of what we might consider to be the major events in human history are passed over without mention, in fact, apart from prophetic statements no events in human history after AD 100 are mentioned. In that sense, all of modern history is passed over. The major focus of the 40 plus authors concerns the period from 2100 BC, the call of Abraham (Gen 12:1-3) to AD 95, the writing of the book of Revelation.[3] The writers focus on some events that may seem inconsequential to us and yet ignore many events that we might consider worthy of mention. For example, I often hear people ask, "Is the United States in prophecy?" Of course, the answer is "no," at least not directly. But the question reveals that we tend to be myopic, viewing things from our own historical perspective. To us, the U.S. seems like an important world power, perhaps having greater power and wealth than any other nation in history, so why would it not be mentioned in prophecy? Simply because the focus of the biblical writers is on something else.

Many major lands and countries are not even named, while one small little country is the center stage and laser-like focus of most all of the biblical writers. Why? Precisely because this book (the Bible) is not primarily man-centered. Man is a major character but not the only character. There are animals, angels, and, of course, most obviously, God. This shows us that the writers were not concerned with what modern day historians might deem most important. The focus of the biblical writers was not what we might identify as major world events, but rather they honed-in on nations and events only as they intersected with God's unfolding plan. Thus, the Bible is man-centered only to the degree that man plays a major part in God's unfolding drama. Though the lives of many characters are revealed, most of what we would find in a modern-day biography is missing because the biblical authors were primarily interested in these lives not for the lives themselves, but as they related to and intersected God's unfolding purposes.

Is it a book about salvation?

If the Bible was philosophically a man-centered book, we might

---

3   I realize that many scholars hold to an earlier date of the writing of the last book of the Bible, but that does not affect the point I am making here.

expect the personal salvation of man to be its main or dominant topic. It is true that a major focus of the Bible, from Genesis 3 through Revelation 20, is the historical unfolding plan of God in providing salvation through the death and resurrection of his Messiah. Yet as important as this is, the content the of the books of the Old Testament reveal to us that relatively little is written about the death of the Messiah when compared to the passages that project his prophesied rule. Of course, the New Testament has a greater focus on the theme of the Messiah's death and resurrection. A major section of each of the Gospels is dedicated to that topic. But even then, at least two thirds of the Gospel material is about the Messiah's personhood and ministry apart from His passion. The Bible emphasizes the redemption of man but that is not all that God is doing in history, nor is it even the supreme goal in God's purpose. A more encompassing subject is the historical advancement of God's kingdom program on the earth, which includes salvation, judgment, and His millennial rule.

A book about God's plan to redeem and to rule for His glory

All the events of human history find their source in the past eternal plans of God "who works all things according to the counsel of His will" (Eph 1:11). Some of His purposes do not reach their final fulfillment until the creation of the new heaven and earth (Rev 21–22). Yet even though the eternal heavens and earth are history's final goal, there is a surprising scarcity of revelation about the eternal state until we come to the Bible's final two chapters. Rather, most of its content focuses on the historical unfolding and outworking of God's purpose on this earth.[4] The original creation mandate was to fill and subdue the earth (Gen

---

4   Of the 1,189 chapters in the Bible, only two deal with the original creation (Gen 1–2), and except for a few scattered statements only two other chapters (Rev 21–22) deal specifically and exclusively with eternity. However, I realize that for some expositors and Bible students, this percentage is larger because they interpret many prophetic passages as referring to the eternal state that I would perhaps categorize as texts referring to a millennial setting.

1:28). The ability to achieve this goal was greatly thwarted by the fall of the human race into sin (Gen 3). But through God's Messiah, mankind is enabled to regain the earth and fulfill the original commission (Heb 2:5-10; Rev 20:4). The redemption of men and women plays a major part in God's purpose, but it is not the final goal of it. Rather, redemption becomes the means by which the redeemed are prepared to co-rule with the Messiah over the creation and on into eternal state (Matt 19:28; 1 Cor 6:2-3; 15:24-28; Rev 5:9-10; 20:4; 22:5). The actual content of the books of the Bible, particularly the narrative portions, chronicle the historical development of God's work on the earth, in relation to the salvation he procures, and the preparation for the Messiah's rule, both on the earth and in eternity.

Unfortunately, many theologies highlight salvation or the redemptive purpose of God to the neglect of his purpose in ruling. As the death of Christ has often been preached to the neglect of the resurrection, so also the initial coming of the king and has been often taught to the neglect of his coming in glory to rule and reign.

Some expositors might object and argue that the major focus of the Scripture is the redemption of man. From our human perspective that may seem to be the case, but a counterargument can be made that the content and focus of the biblical revelation is not merely the redemption of mankind, for most men and women will not be redeemed. Rather it is both the redemption as well as the restoration of man and the earth for the glory of God. The Apostle Paul emphasizes three times in the first chapter of Ephesians that redemption's purpose is "to the praise of his glory," that is, it serves a greater purpose, God's glory (Eph 1:6, 12, 14).

Though redemption is a major theme in the Bible, it serves a wider and broader goal, God's glory, which involves the reestablishment of His direct rule over the demonic world, mankind, and the earth. Men are redeemed for a purpose, to co-rule with

God forever, beginning in the millennial age and from that point transitioning into the eternal state. More accurately, the focus of the Bible is the recovery of man from the fall. This involves spiritual redemption and a restoration of God's original purpose for man to rule the earth as God's viceregent, as expressed in Psalm 8:4-6,

> What is man that You take thought of him,
> And the son of man that You care for him?
> Yet You have made him a little lower than God,
> And You crown him with glory and majesty!
> You make him to rule over the works of Your hands;
> You have put all things under his feet.

In the New Testament, the author of Hebrews cites this passage, but then adds this very interesting point:

> "For in subjecting all things to him, He left nothing that is not subject to him. *But now we do not yet see all things subjected to him*" (emphasis added, Heb 2:8).

"But now we do not yet see all things subjected to him." This alludes back to the Genesis narrative when God created man to rule and subdue the entire earth. Because of the fall of man and the entrance of sin into the world, this commission was hindered. The writer of Hebrews has observed that all things are "*not yet*" subject to the dominion of man.

The fall of man did not take God by surprise. Since salvation was prepared before the world began (Eph 1:4), God clearly knew of and planned for the Fall, though He did not directly cause it, man did in submitting to the serpent's temptation (Gen 2:17; 3:1-6). Yet ultimately it was a part of God's sovereign purpose to redeem creation for the sake of His and our glory.

For the creation was subjected to futility, not willingly, but because of Him who subjected it, in hope that the creation itself also will be set free from its slavery to corruption into the freedom of the glory of the children of God. (Rom 8:20-21).

So, it appears that God allowed the creation to fall, having a greater purpose of rescuing and renewing it for His glory. His ultimate purpose in all this was His own glory. Paul tells us that God is working "all things according to the counsel of His will" (Eph 1:11) and ultimately to the "praise of His glory" (Eph 1:6, 12, 14). Salvation does benefit man, but its deeper significance is not merely our enjoyment but His glory.

Does the fall of man mean that God has jettisoned His original creation mandate and that mankind will never be able to fulfill God's original commission? Has sinful man and Satan completely frustrated God's original creation purpose? That may currently seem to be the case, as the writer of Hebrews says, "But now we do not yet see all things subjected to him." But, of course, this is not the end of the story.

CHAPTER 1

DOES HUMAN HISTORY HAVE A GOAL?

We often ask ourselves, is there any purpose to human or world history? At times, all seems pointless. For the secular man or woman who steps back and looks at history and even their own life, things do not seem to make much sense. After hearing of the death of his wife, Shakespeare's Macbeth uttered this tragic view of life:

> *Life's but a walking shadow, a poor player,*
> *That struts and frets his hour upon the stage,*
> *And then is heard no more.*
> *It is a tale told by an idiot,*
> *Full of sound and fury,*
> *Signifying nothing.*

Does history signify anything or does it, as Shakespeare's Macbeth emphasize, "signify nothing"? Most of us, at some point in life, have seriously wondered if life is heading anywhere in particular. So much of ancient history seems to make no sense, and modern history does not appear to be moving in any meaningful direction.

In the nineteenth century the philosophy of existentialism emerged which basically said there is no meaning to life, therefore if there is to be any meaning, we must create it ourselves. So, from the standpoint of secular history there is no particular meaning to what has gone before us or what will follow. Even the biblical writer Solomon insightfully expressed this same frustration,

> What advantage does man have in all his work which he does under the sun? A generation goes and a generation comes, but the earth remains forever. Also, the sun rises and the sun sets; and hastening to its place it rises there *again*. Blowing toward the south, then turning toward the north, the wind continues swirling along; and on its circular courses the wind returns. All the rivers flow into the sea, yet the sea is not full. To the place where the rivers flow, there they flow again. All things are wearisome; man is not able to tell *it*...(Eccl 1:3-8).

IS THERE A GOAL WITHIN HISTORY?

Solomon's observations truthfully expressed his feelings about life as he saw it. From a merely human perspective, life and history seem to have no particular purpose or goal. But from the divine perspective, only accessible through revelation, life does have meaning and history is going somewhere, somewhere very, very specific. This is the central conviction of the Bible. The content of the Bible chronicles the historical movement towards this goal.

We would not and could not know where the world is heading if God had not made it a matter of revelation. But He has made it a matter of revelation—a revelation that has come through forty plus authors and over a period of more than 1500 years. Though not every biblical author spoke directly to this particular topic, those that did were of one mind regarding it. World history has one glorious goal towards which it is rapidly moving. The goal I am referring to is not only the new heaven and new earth. Eternity stands outside of history and logically follows the goal God has for *this* world. The Bible projects a goal in time, within earth's history. This seems to be what the overwhelming content of the Bible concerns itself with and is moving towards.

We might pose the question this way: If the new heaven and earth are God's final goal for redeemed humanity, what might be His specific goal for mankind within redemptive history on this earth? The reason I pose this question is because the content of the Bible covers, almost exclusively, the unfolding of God's work in human history, from the time from the fall of man up to the point when the new heaven and earth are created. By way of contrast, little space is given to describe the final state, even though that is our ultimate hope. We in the church might answer the question above saying, "The highest purpose of history or its highest goal is to get the message of the gospel to the ends of the earth so that as many people as possible might come to experience salvation through faith in the Messiah." This is surely part of the church's commission (Matt 28:19-20). In fact, one reason that Christ has not yet returned is because God is giving the church the time needed to carry out that commission not desiring that any perish (2 Pet 3:9). Yet the church, which began at Acts 2 and ends when Christ comes for his bride, only covers a portion of human history. It is a significant part of God's work, but when we back up to view the totality of Scripture, the church and its mission comprises only part of what God has done and will do.

The narrative story of the Bible focuses on redemptive history leading up to the death and resurrection of the Messiah, but as mentioned earlier, it is noteworthy that relatively few chapters describe in detail his death and resurrection. Rather, the greater focus, particularly in the prophetic Scriptures seems to be on the judgment the Messiah brings at specific times in history and particularly at its end, which then leads to his direct rule over the earth. Why is there more space given to describe His judgment and rule than His redemption when both are supremely important? Because in the Scripture God is revealing to us where human history is headed. Early on, the Bible address the theme of Messianic redemption for it is announced immediately after the fall of man into sin (Gen 3:15), but the Scripture ends with a focus on the rule and reign of the Messiah on the earth with His redeemed (cf. Rev 5:10; 11:15; 20:1-10). Within history the climactic goal is the direct rule and reign of the Messiah. Over the years, as I have continued to read through the entire Bible over and over again, I begin to see ever more clearly that its content moves ever so slowly towards this ultimate goal and dramatic climax.

Admittedly, once the earth is regained in Revelation 19 (the Second Coming of Christ), little space is devoted in chapter 20 to chronicle his rule, though a thousand-year period is mentioned six times there. However, the prophetic Scriptures of the Old Testament as well as the Psalmists give abundant information about this glorious coming kingdom.

Although God is of course very concerned about eternity and our final destination, as I mentioned, only two chapters in Revelation describe the eternal state in any detail. The sheer volume of material in the rest of the Bible that chronicles this historical movement from the loss of paradise to the point where Messiah rules the earth reveals to us the particular focus and interest of the biblical writers. The biblical writers emphasize not only the process of procuring salvation, but also Messiah's climactic return and rule with those He redeems. The Messiah's purpose was not only to redeem a people for His name, but also to bring them into His rule,

You have made them *to be* a kingdom and priests to our God; and they will reign upon the earth. (Rev 5:10).

It is through this redemption and Messianic reign that the original creation purpose will be achieved. Man will "Be fruitful and multiply, and fill the earth, and subdue it; and rule over the fish of the sea and over the birds of the sky and over every living thing that moves on the earth," albeit under the rule of Christ (Gen 1:28; Heb 2:7-10). God's purpose for this earth will be fulfilled and Satan will have been defeated. In the following pages I want to unpack the chronological movement in history towards this goal.

THE FAILURE OF HUMAN GOVERNMENTS

From a divine perspective, human history (from original Babylon in Gen 11 to Babylon's final appearance in Rev 17–18), reveals that no man or government is able or worthy to rule over the disputed and contended territory of planet Earth. Every imaginable or feasible form of rule has been tried, and they all eventually fall short of the aspirations of both man and God. At their worst, human governments engage in persecution and injustice, even genocide. History proves to men and angels that there is only One who is worthy and able to reign justly over the earth (Rev 5:9). He alone will show to the human world and angelic realm what it means to rule the world in righteousness. Scripture teaches that He will defeat His enemies, conquer the world, and regain the earth. He will rule it with a "rod of iron" (Ps 2:9; Rev 2:27; 12:5; 19:15). God and His Messiah will be finally vindicated on the earth.

Despite the number of passages that reinforce this truth, much of the church for many centuries has relegated this promise entirely to the church age or to the eternal state. Basically, they have argued that Jesus' prayer for the kingdom to come "on earth as it is in heaven" is being fulfilled now in the church or it is a request that will be fulfilled in the eternal state when God fashions the new heaven and a new earth (cf. Matt 6:10; Rev 21:1). Those applications may be true in part, but numerous passages also depict a kingdom that is coming to this earth, after the church and before the new heaven and earth are fashioned.

The coming of this kingdom to earth within human history is the goal towards which the Bible and human history inexorably move,

> Let the heavens be glad, and let the earth rejoice;
> Let the sea roar, and all it contains;
> Let the field exult, and all that is in it.
> Then all the trees of the forest will sing for joy.
> Before the LORD, for He is coming,
> For He is coming to judge the earth.
> He will judge the world in righteousness.
> And the peoples in His faithfulness (Ps 96:11-13).

How sure is this goal? The writer of Hebrews declares when God wanted to assure Abraham that His covenant was immutable, He swore by Himself because there was no greater authority in the universe, and no *being* more faithful than God himself. It is impossible for Him to lie (cf. Titus 1:2; Heb 6:13-18). In the Old Testament one of the tests of a true prophet was the truthfulness of his predictions. Did his prophecies come true? If not, he was considered a false prophet deserving the death penalty (Deut 18:15-22). If all that God has promised and predicted in His word does not come true, then He would not only be a false prophet but also a false God.

The trustworthiness of God is at stake. Did God say what He meant? Is He able to bring it to pass? In the Old Testament prophesies regarding the goal of human history and the coming reign of the Messiah, did He mean what He said? It is a question of the character of God. Or did Israel's unbelief defeat His purpose? Does He annul His promises, or not communicate them clearly? Paul's answer is that "the gifts and the calling of God are irrevocable" (Rom 11:29). When we say the Messiah will be vindicated on earth, it is the promises that God made that will be vindicated and fulfilled. His faithfulness depends upon it. He will be glorified by these fulfillments because both men and angels will marvel when they see Him bring to fruition the very things, He promised thousands of years ago.

CHAPTER 2

OLD TESTAMENT KINGDOM DEVELOPMENTS AND THE MAJOR COVENANTS

W hen we consider the narrative backbone of the Old Testament, the individual pericopes and narrative stories, they seem to be designed for at least three important purposes. First, to reveal the person and character of God, second, to nurture the faith of His people through God's interaction with the main characters and their responses to God, and third, to reveal to His people His unfolding plan at any particular point in history. This plan is not brought to completion in the Old Testament, but it is there that it begins, builds, and develops. The thrust of the plan is ultimately to redeem men and women from every tribe and nation and language, and to bring God's purpose for the earth to its intended goal—a kingdom where man rules under God.

By surveying the narrative drama presented to us in the Old Testament, we can begin to see what God is doing in this world and where history is heading. This can be demonstrated though a survey of selected portions of Scripture.

MAN'S ORIGINAL COMMISSION

In Genesis 1, Moses records for us the original creation account in which he characterizes God's work as "good" no less than seven times, the seventh time as "very good" (Gen 1:4,10,12,18, 21, 25, 31). God commissioned the human race with the words, "Be fruitful and multiply and fill the earth and subdue it and have dominion over the fish of the sea and over the birds of the heavens and over every living thing that moves on the earth" (Gen 1:28). In Genesis 2 God planted a garden in Eden where He placed Adam and created Eve. In God's command for Adam to "keep" the garden, the word "keep" is often translated in other places in the Old Testament as "guard." The charge to guard the garden already intimated that its pristine condition and moral purity could be compromised or threatened from the outside. This implied that evil was already on the loose in the universe— though it was not yet present on the earth. Thus, man's dominion had been established and his rule began in Eden and was to gradually extend to the entire earth.

THE FALL AND SUBSEQUENT PROMISE OF BLESSING

Genesis 3 chronicles the tragic fall of the human race into sin (cf. Gen 3:1-6; Rom 5:12). It was through the serpent's temptation of Eve and Adam's blatant disobedience to God that the fall occurred (Gen 2:17; 3:1-6). The original state of blessing bestowed upon the creation was lost. As a result, man's physical, moral, and spiritual ability to carry out the original creation mandate to fill and subdue the earth and to rule over the animal world was in put jeopardy.

Satan had directly challenged God's right to rule. God could have destroyed Satan at once, or He could have destroyed his first creation and started anew. But that is not what He chose to do. Rather, He planned for man to continue to multiply, albeit now in a sinful state, and He allows the Devil to exercise some degree of dominion over the world.

Satan had usurped God's direct rule of the earth, becoming the "god of this world" and soon to be deceiver of the nations (2 Cor 4:4; Rev 20:3). He assumed that he had won the right to rule the world. We see this assumption later in the New Testament when he tells Christ that he had been given authority over the kingdoms of the earth,

> And the devil took him up and showed him all the kingdoms of the world in a moment of time, and said to him, "To you I will give all this authority and their glory, for it has been delivered to me, and I give it to whom I will. If you, then, will worship me, it will all be yours." (Luke 4:5-7).

Satan's rebellion and man's fall in no way impugns God sovereign control of all things, including this earth and Satan himself. As we have already noted, God had allowed his creation to fall into sin because through it he planned to carry out his glorious purpose in redemption and restoration.

> For the creation was subjected to futility, not willingly, but because of him who subjected it, in hope that the creation itself will be set free from its bondage to corruption and obtain the freedom of the glory of the children of God (Rom 8:20-21).

His plan would be to redeem multitudes of men and women, restore his creation, and bring to completion his purposes for mankind on the earth. This plan would not take place at once but rather it would be progressive in nature, unfolding in and through human history.

This hope implied that God would not allow the world in its fallen condition to go on forever. World history would not end as a disastrous divine experiment. Rather, subsequent revelation in the Bible shows us that God will redeem multitudes of men and women, defeat his foe (Satan) and climatically install his Messiah as ruler over all the earth.

A millennial worldview maintains that the climax of human history will be the foiling of Satan's insurrection in this world—not just in the sense that God has made a way for multitudes to enter heaven, but even more poignant is the fact that God will vindicate his Messiah on the earth. The kingdoms of "this world" will become the kingdoms of "his Christ" (Rev 11:15). Even more astonishing is that we will reign with him "on the earth" (Rev 5:10). This was Jesus' prayer in Matthew 6:10, "Thy will be done on earth as it is in heaven."

The abject failure and corruption of human kingdoms and rulers throughout world history display the truth that God's Messiah alone is worthy and able to rule the earth (Rev 5:12). Thus, we can rightly assume that his rule on earth will be an unsurpassed revelation of his glory. The whole realm of creation belongs to him—including this fallen earth—and it will again come under his direct dominion. But even at that time, since it will still be fallen, He must rule it with "a rod of iron" (Rev 2:27).

From Genesis 3 on, we begin to see God's unfolding plan to bring mankind back under the influence of His blessing, in part so that He could fulfill the original creation mandate. The first hint of this restoration is introduced in Genesis 3:15 where God, speaking judgment against the serpent who had tempted Adam and Eve to disobey, said, "He shall bruise you on the head, and you shall bruise him on the heel." Satan would be bruised on the head, a reference to a fatal blow. It is noteworthy that Christ defeated Satan at the cross (Col 2:14-15; Heb 2:14) and at the end of the Bible Satan is first imprisoned for 1000 years, and then cast into the lake of fire for eternity (Rev 20:3, 10). The writer of Hebrews confirmed that through the Messiah's death he would "render powerless him who had the power of death, that is, the devil" (Heb 2:14). The one who would bring this defeat would be bruised on the heal, a non-fatal blow. That individual is not yet identified in Genesis 3:15, but it becomes clear in subsequent revelation that it is a reference to Jesus, the Messiah (see Ps 22:16; Isa 53:5: Zech 12:10; Rom 16:20; Rev 12:9).

THE CREATION MANDATE AFTER THE FLOOD

Part of the original creation commission was repeated after the Noahic flood, "God blessed Noah and his sons and said to them, 'Be fruitful and multiply, and fill the earth'" (Gen 9:1). In the original commission, God had also commanded mankind to rule over "the fish of the sea and over the birds of the sky and over every living thing that moves on the earth" (Gen 1:28). But now He introduces a new component in man's relationship to the animal kingdom. He implants a fear of man in "every beast of the earth and on every bird of the sky; with everything that creeps on the ground, and all the fish of the sea,"—a fear that the animal kingdom apparently did not possess before the Flood (Gen 9:2).

In addition, mankind was now allowed to eat the flesh of animals as food yet forbidden to drink their blood (Gen 9:3-4). So, the original commission was not rescinded by the fall or the Flood, but rather restated with some modification. God then seals this arrangement with a covenant between himself, every human descendant and "every living creature" summarized as "all flesh" (Gen 9:9-17). The main point to see at this point in history, is that the original creation mandate was largely still in effect.

THE ABRAHAMIC COVENANT

The Abrahamic covenant is an outgrowth of the original promise of victory over Satan that will be accomplished through the Messiah (Gen 3:15). It is one of the most important covenants in the Old Testament. In many aspects it was both unilateral and unconditional and thus cannot be abrogated. Abraham was put to sleep when God made it (Gen 15:12-21; 17:7). This indicates that fulfillment of the covenant ultimately depends not on Abraham or his descendants' obedience but rather on God's faithfulness.

Before the actual covenant ceremony takes place in Genesis 15, God makes seven statements to Abraham in Genesis 12:1-3 which can be condensed into three basic promises:

1. **A land** where the covenant will be realized (Gen 12:1). Later, the borders of the land were clearly and repeatedly delineated (Gen 12:7; 13:14; 15:18-21).

2. **A great nation** of descendants, who would become the Jewish people (the nation of Israel) though whom the Messiah would descend (Gen 12:2; Matt 1:1-17; Rom 1:1-3). The promise of Israel becoming a great nation was repeated several times in Genesis (Gen 12:2; 13:16, 18; 17:2-5; 22:17).

3. **National and universal blessing** (which refers ultimately to spiritual salvation procured by the Messiah) was repeated several times (Gen 12:2-3; 18:8; 22:18; 26:4).

It is noteworthy that part of the Abrahamic promise is that "kings" shall come forth from Abraham (Gen 17:6-7). This promise opens the door for the possibility that one of these kings will be the Messiah who will descend through Abraham's son Isaac (Gen17:21; 21:12). At the end of the book of Genesis, the author speaks about the future of the twelve tribes of Israel. Regarding the tribe of Judah (the name derived from one of Jacob's sons), he declares, "The scepter shall not depart from Judah, nor the ruler's staff from between his feet, until Shiloh comes, and to him shall be the obedience of the peoples" (Gen 49:10). This ruler will come from the line of Judah and his rule will be over all "the peoples." The word "Shiloh" probably means "the one to whom it belongs" or possibly it is a name for the Messiah meaning "peace." The description of his prosperity in verses 11-12, describes an earthly setting. Thus, the expectation is that this ruler will reign over the land granted to Abraham's descendants.

The rest of the Old Testament and the Gospels of the New Testament focus on God's dealings with the descendants of Abraham. Other Gentile nations have only an ancillary role as their history intersects with Israel. The purpose behind the formation of the nation of Israel is so that God can bring all mankind under the influence of his blessing that was lost at the fall (cf. Gen 3:1-19; 12:1-3). Abraham and his descendants, particularly one specific descendant, Christ (Gal 3:16), would be God's primary instrument through whom he would channel his blessing to all the nations of the world (John 4:22; Gal 3:29). Historically, the response of the nations to Abraham and his descendants would reflect their response to God (Gen 12:3).

It is not an exaggeration to say that the Abrahamic covenant is the foundation to all that God promised and will bring to pass for Israel and the nations of the earth, encompassing the plan of salvation and the establishment of his kingdom. Both the Davidic (2 Sam 7:12-16) and New Covenants (Jer 31:31-37; Ezek 37:26) find their source in this covenant.

This covenant lays the foundation for the coming Messianic rule. The land is the focal point from where the Messiah will rule, the physical descendants are the Jewish people that comprise the original recipients of the promise, though the Messiah's realm will also include multitudes of spiritual descendants from the nations as well (Gal 3:16, 26-29). The blessing is the salvation that they will all enjoy.

THE MOSAIC COVENANT

Thus far we have seen the prediction of One who would defeat Satan (Gen 3:15), the promise of a coming of a ruler (Gen 49:10), and the pledge that Abraham's offspring would become the source of blessing for the entire world (Gen 12:1-3).

The second book of the Bible, Exodus, explains how the Abrahamic family became a nation (Exod 1:1-7). God created the nation by supernaturally redeeming and delivering it from slavery in Egypt (Exod. 1–18). He then established his rule among them by giving them the Law (Exod 19–24) and revealed to them the way of worship through the priesthood and tabernacle (Exod 25–40). God's intervention in Egypt arose in fulfillment of his promise to Abraham to give his descendants the land of Canaan (Gen 15:13-14; Exod 2:24-25; 3:8).

In Exodus 19–24, Moses records the giving of the Law which regulated the relationship of the nation to God. This signaled the formal beginning of the Jewish nation and set Israel apart from the other nations. God first revealed that his purpose for them was that they would serve as a "kingdom of priests" (Exod 19:5-6). This is not a reference to the priesthood within the nation but to the nation as a whole, since they are all designated as priests. Ostensibly, Israel would serve as a mediating nation between God and the Gentile nations (Exod 19:5-6; Deut 4:6). This ministry by the nation of Israel will probably not be completely realized until the millennial reign of the Messiah. The nation verbally agreed to enter into this covenant (Exod 19:7-8), which was sealed by a blood sacrifice (Exod 24:7-8).

The Book of Exodus closes with God taking up His residence among the nation as their physically present ruler (Exod 40:34-38). Succinctly stated, the book of Exodus reveals how the Abrahamic family grew to be a nation governed by God through the Mosaic Law. In addition, Exodus reveals to the nation how they were to approach God, by means of the priesthood at the tabernacle.

16

TAKING THE LAND

After forty years of disobedience and discipline in the desert, the nation is finally ready to take possession of their promised homeland, the land of Canaan, from where God will launch his plan to bless *all* nations (Gen 12:3).

Through Moses and Joshua, God had commissioned the nation to take all the land of Canaan (Exod 23:20–30; Num 33:50–56, Deut 7:1–6). The nation had agreed to obey God in this effort (Josh 1:13–16). Under Joshua's leadership they drove out many of the Canaanites and distributed the land to the twelve tribes of Israel.

On the one hand, God had fully delivered on his promise to give them the land by aiding them in holy warfare (cf. Gen 12:2-3, 7; 13:15; 15:18-21; 17:8; 26:3; 28:13; Josh 21:43-45; 23:14; 24:13). On the other hand, the nation did not *fully* conquer all the land to the extent of its promised boarders but failed to follow through on completely eradicating all those dwelling in the land[5] (cf. Gen 15:18-21; Exod 23:31; Num 13:21; Deut 11:24; Josh 13:1-7; 16:10; 17:12-13; 23:1-5; Judg 1:27-2:4). Thus, many geographical pockets of Canaanites remained scattered throughout the land (Josh 13:1-7; Judg 1:27–2:4). In fact, Israel has never fully possessed, without interruption, all the land promised in the Abrahamic covenant (cf. Gen 12:7; 13:14; 15:18-21; Num 34; Josh 13–18). This is an important point because it means the promises God made to the nation still await a final fulfillment.

---

5   The justification behind the eradication of the Canaanites was that they practiced gross immorality to the point of sacrificing their children to pagan gods (Lev 18:21; Deut 9:4-5; 12:29-31). God gave them over 700 years to repent (from the time of Abraham to the time of Moses), but they refused to do so (Gen 15:16). In the case where even one would repent, such as Rehab, God graciously delivered her and her family from judgment (cf. Josh 2:17-20; 6:22-23). Failure to eradicate the Canaanites led Israel to worship their gods just as God predicted (cf. Deut 7:2-5; 20:17-18; 2 Kgs 17:8-18).

THE RISE AND FALL OF THE MONARCHY IN ISRAEL

Under the Judges the nation functioned as a loose confederacy for at least three hundred years without a centralized government. Beginning with Saul, the promised monarchy was implemented (Gen 17:6; Deut 17:14-15; 1 Sam 9:15-17; 10:1, 10; 15:17). The early reproach against the nation for wanting a king was not due to God never planning for there to be a monarchy but because the Hebrews wanted the king in Israel to be like the monarchies of the surrounding pagan nations (1 Sam 8:4-7; 12:12). God's purposes and timing for the monarchy were different than Israel's (Deut 17:14-20; 1 Sam 13:14). The establishment of the monarchy had always been a part of God's plan. This was first seen in the fact that He promised a ruler would come from Judah (Gen 49:10) and kings would descend from Abraham's line (Gen 17:6). The regulations given in Deuteronomy 17 for the kings to follow demonstrates that there was a divine intention to implement a monarchy in the nation. It prepared the way for the coming of the Messianic King (cf. 2 Sam 7:12-13, 16; Luke 1:31-33).

One of the things that the nearly 500-year period of Israel's monarchy demonstrates is that no human king was of the moral and spiritual stature to adequately represent God's rule on earth. This can be deduced by observing a brief survey of the monarchy given below.

THE DAVIDIC COVENANT (2 SAM 7:14–16).

After Saul's sin and rejection, David was chosen to rule Israel. The high point of God's purpose in implementing the kingship was revealed in 2 Samuel 7:8–16 where He established an eternal covenant with David, promising a house (cf. 2 Sam 7:1; Luke 1:33), a throne (2 Sam 7:13; Luke 1:32), and a kingdom over which he and his descendant(s) would rule (cf. 2 Sam 7:1; Luke 1:33).

The Highpoint of the Kingdom

The kingship in Israel approached its ideal in David and Solomon, but fell short of its ultimate goal, the rule of righteousness. David's moral sin disrupted the kingdom and brought him troubles the rest of his reign but did not nullify the covenant God made with him for it was an unconditional promise (cf. 2 Sam 7:15; 12:9-13; 22:48).

Following David, for a brief moment in history, the nation rose to a place of splendor in the world under the rule of Solomon. When he began his rule, the kingdom in Israel had reached the apex of its influence and prosperity. There was virtually no military threat from her neighbors, "Judah and Israel *were* as numerous as the sand that is on the seashore in abundance; *they* were eating and drinking and rejoicing" (1 Kgs 4:20).

Solomon oversaw the building of the temple. In his prayer of dedication, he recognized that Israel, of all the nations of the earth was unique in God's purpose (1 Kgs 8:53, 60). Just as God's glory had filled the tabernacle at the time of the Exodus, so now at the time of Solomon it also filled the temple indicating the continuation of the theocracy in Israel and signifying God presence in the temple (Exod 40:34-38; 2 Chron 7:1-3).

Solomon's polygamy led him into the worship of many gods and began the downward spiral of the monarchy in Israel.

The Decline of the Kingdom in Israel and Judah

The years of the monarchy in Israel can be divided into three distinguishable periods:

1. The unified kingdom under Saul, David, and Solomon (1 Sam 10–1 Kgs 10)

2. The divided kingdoms of Israel and Judah (1 Kgs 11–2 Kgs 17)

3. The surviving kingdom of Judah (2 Kgs 18–25)

The Kingdom remained united under Saul, David and Solomon (1 Sam 10–1 Kgs 10). But following Solomon, the Kingdom divided into the north and south and began a rapid decline (Solomon's reign began in 971 BC, the split took place just forty years later in 931 BC). After the division of the kingdom, God no longer selected the kings as He had done with Saul, David, and Solomon. However, the kingdom rule continued through the Davidic line in the Southern Kingdom of Judah (cf. Gen 49:10; 1 Kgs 11:11-13). By way of summary, Israel had nineteen kings, all were evil. Judah had twenty kings, twelve were evil and eight were good.

THE END OF THE THEOCRATIC KINGDOM IN ISRAEL

From the time of Solomon's engagement in polygamy and idolatry (1 Kgs 11) until the Assyrian and Babylonian captivities (2 Kgs 17; 24-25), Israel experienced a progressive spiritual and moral decline by departing from the Law of Moses and engaging in gross idolatry.

The Assyrian Captivity

As a judgment and as a discipline stipulated in the law, Israel (the ten northern tribes) was taken captive to Assyria in 722 BC (cf. Lev 26:27-33; Deut 28:63; 2 Kgs 17:5-6). The Assyrians repopulated the area and inter-married with the Jews (2 Kgs 17:24-25, 29-34). The offspring of these marriages were called Samaritans (cf. John 4).

The Babylonian Captivity

More than a hundred years later, Judah and Benjamin (the Southern Kingdom) where the line of David continued, were taken captive to Babylon in three phases: (1) the royalty was taken in 605 BC (e.g. Dan 1:1-4); (2) the general population was taken in 597 BC (2 Kgs 24:10–16); and (3) the rest of the people were taken in 586 BC (2 Kgs 25:8–12). The city and temple were burned (2 Kgs 25:9).

The prophet Jeremiah was an eyewitness to the events surrounding the destruction of Jerusalem by the Babylonians (2 Kgs 24–25; Jer 39–52). In the book of Lamentations he records the trauma of the Babylonian deportations to remind the survivors of the high cost of sin. He is careful to reveal two things about God. First, although He is slow to judge, He will in no way withhold judgment of sin from those who will not repent. He is serious about sin and his judgment can seem merciless. Second, the severe judgment of God will never negate his promises or his compassionate character. Thus, the promises of God made to Abraham and David had not been abrogated or annulled.

THE DEPARTURE OF THE GLORY OF GOD

One of the signs of God's theocratic kingdom on earth was the presence of His glory. It was probably present at creation, described as the "presence of the Lord" which Adam and Eve saw after their fall into sin (Gen 3:8). When Adam and Eve were blocked from the tree of life after their fall into sin, cherubim with a flaming sword were placed there to block their access. Cherubim are often associated with God's glory (cf. Ezek 1; 8–11).

The manifestation of God's glory first appeared to the children of Israel in the pillar of cloud that led them out of Egypt (Exod 13:20-22). It shone forth from within the cloud (Exod 16:7, 10) and had the appearance of a consuming fire (Exod 24:16). Later, Moses requested to see God's glory (Exod 33:18). God agreed but warned that no man could see his face (the fullness of his glory) and live (Exod 33:20). God hid Moses in a cleft of a rock and covered him with his hand so that he would not be consumed by the glory He showed him.

God's glory filled the tabernacle and accompanied the Israelites throughout their wilderness wanderings (Exod 13:20-21; 40:34-38). Several times it appeared as a prelude to God's judgment. Later, at the time of King Solomon, God's glory also entered the temple (1 Kgs 8:10-13; 2 Chron 7:1-3). It was still present in the temple just prior to the Babylonian captivity (Ezek 8:1-4). Ezekiel cites idolatry as one of the major reasons for its departure (Ezek 8:8-15). The prophet carefully traced its departure from Israel. God's glory resided in the holy of holies of the temple, above the wings of the cherubim which were positioned on each side of the cover to the Ark of the Covenant. The glory first left from above the cherubim and went to the temple doorway, illuminating the courtyard (Ezek 9:3, 10:3-4,18-19). From there, the glory went up from the city, rested upon the Mount of Olives, then finally departed the city (Ezek 11:22-23). The theocratic kingdom in Israel came to an end when the Davidic line was taken captive to Babylon and the glory of God representing his special presence departed from the temple. However the promises of rule were not nullified.

The kings that God promised would come from Abraham's descendants did indeed come (Gen 17:6), but because of their sin they all fell short of successfully establishing God's rule on earth. The question arises, if the monarchy in Israel failed, how will God fulfill his promise of bringing a great king into the world who will one day rule the earth? How will God's glory and his blessing be reestablished on the earth?

This period of the absence of the monarchy in Israel is referred to as "the time of the Gentiles" because it is the period when God's immediate presence, and glory are absent, and Israel is subject to or dominated by Gentile powers (cf. Dan 2; 7; Luke 21:24, Rom 11:25). The period began with the Babylonian captivity and appears to end at the second coming of Christ when Jesus returns in power and glory (Matt 24:30). Two of Daniel's visions, his vision of the statue and his vision of the beasts coming out of the sea, cover this period of Gentile domination over Israel (Dan 2:1-43; 7:1-25). The empires delineated there are Babylon, Persia, Greece, and Rome. Jesus refers to the time of the Gentiles in the Olivet Discourse where he says, "Jerusalem will be trampled underfoot by the Gentiles until the times of the Gentiles are fulfilled" (Luke 21:24). Clearly all this history is part of God's plan.

The history of the monarchy in Israel reveals that the nation needed a ruler who was divinely powerful to put down all rebellion, yet also morally and spiritually perfect so as to please God. This ideal will not be realized until the Messiah rules in the kingdom of God, fulfilling the promises made to Abraham and David.

There were two major reasons for the collapse of the theocratic kingdom in Israel. and the departure of his glory. First, Israel wanted to have a monarchy so that they could be like the nations, "They said, 'No, but there shall be a king over us, that we also may be like all the nations,'" (1 Sam 8:19-20). This was in opposition to God's purpose for the monarchy. Second, Israel departed from the Mosaic Law, becoming wealthy, proud, and idolatrous (2 Kgs 17:6-18).

THE POST-EXILIC COMMUNITY

The author of 1 and 2 Kings, traditionally believed to be Jeremiah, probably wrote to those Jews who were living in the Babylonian captivity to remind them of why they had experienced God's judgment. By way of contrast, the writer of 1 and 2 Chronicles, traditionally believed to be Ezra, covered some of the same historical period but most likely wrote to those Jews that had returned to the land after the captivities. Thus, he had a different emphasis. He emphasized the greatness of the former kingdom in Judah from which God had promised to make an eternal kingdom through the line of David. This returning remnant was encouraged to reestablish, propagate, and protect the proper worship of God in Israel—ostensibly until the rightful king or Messiah arrived.

The priests and governors had the immediate task of encouraging the people to rebuild the temple and lead them in the worship of God. But here was no direction by God to reestablish the kingship. This, in part, explains the focus on the ministry of the Levites in 1 and 2 Chronicles and later in the book of Ezra. The author wanted to emphasize the importance of their offices and ministries since the monarchy was not going to be reestablished at that time.

It is also noteworthy that the glory of God, which had departed the temple at the time of the Babylonian captivity (Ezek 8–11), did not return to indwell the rebuilt temple in the post-exilic period (Hag 2:3). Also, the Ark of the Covenant was absent. However, the Davidic line continued unbroken through and after the captivity. Zerubbabel was of the seed of David and his line led directly to Christ (Matt 1:12-16).

Though the Messiah did not materialize as one of the kings of Israel or Judah, the prophets nevertheless had proclaimed his coming throughout the Old Testament. At least part of God's purpose during this period may have been as Paul mentions, he was waiting until the "fullness of time" had arrived to bring his Messiah into the world (Gal 4:4).

THE MINISTRY OF THE PROPHETS

The ministry of prophets began as early as Enoch, the fifth generation from Adam (Gen 5:21-23; Jude 14). Abraham was described as a prophet (Gen 20:7) and Moses compared himself to a prophet (Deut 18:15). But it was during Israel's and Judah's spiritual and moral decline that God began to send prophets to the kings and the nation for the purpose of calling them to repentance and warning of impending judgment.

The standard by which the prophets condemned the kings was the Mosaic Law. The nation had entered into a covenant with God, and for God to uphold His end of the agreement, He not only obligated himself to bless the nation when it was obedient, but He also to promised to bring judgment when they were disobedient. The prophets continually reminded the nation of this arrangement.

Another important component of the prophets' ministry was to reveal God's future purpose for the nation. As the nation was spiraling downward, God continued to remind them not only of coming judgment but also of a final glorious fulfillment of all his promises. This involved the promise of the restoration of the kingdom under the Messiah who would fulfill the Abrahamic and Davidic covenants.

The Old Testament prophets prophesied a composite picture of a coming Messiah. He would both suffer in humiliation and yet reign over the whole earth in justice and righteousness. The Old Testament passages that view the Messiah as ruling monarch far outnumber those that portray his lowliness, humiliation, and suffering. Because it was difficult to reconcile the contrasting portraits, and because the Warrior-King view of the Messiah dominated the messianic passages, God's people naturally expected the Messiah to be a conquering ruling king.

Another reason they expected a warrior-king was because they were dominated by Gentile nations and hoping the coming Messiah would deliver them. Thus, when Jesus arrived as a common and humble man, he was outrightly rejected as the possible Messiah. Having the perspective of the New Testament, we are able to deduce that the Messiah would come twice, first as a humble savior, and then again as a conquering king.

The fact that so many passages focus on the Messiah as a conquering warrior makes it clear that God purpose for the Messiah to rule is a least equally important as His purpose was for Him to suffer and die. For example, in Isaiah 9:6-7 only the initial phrase refers to the Messiah's lowliness and death "For a child will be born to us, a son will be given to us." The rest of the passage projects His earthly reign as king:

> And the government will rest on His shoulders; and His name will be called Wonderful Counselor, Mighty God, Eternal Father, Prince of Peace. There will be no end to the increase of His government or of peace, on the throne of David and over his kingdom, to establish it and to uphold it with justice and righteousness from then on and forevermore (Isa 9:6-7).

The biblical writers held a firm conviction that one of God's major purposes for this earth was to set his Son on his throne in Jerusalem, which Isaiah called "the throne of David." Some three hundred years before the time of Isaiah, the Psalmist had already prophesied of this, "But as for Me, I have installed My King upon Zion [Jerusalem], my holy mountain" (Ps 2:6). From there his rule is said to reach to the ends of the earth, "May He also rule from sea to sea and from the River (Euphrates) to the ends of the earth" (Ps 72:8). Announcements of this coming king begin early in the Scripture and build in scope and detail throughout.

CHAPTER 3

IDENTIFYING THE RIGHTFUL RULER

The initial observation regarding the Messiah that the first writer of Scripture makes is that he will be of human origin. In a statement made by God to the serpent after the fall of Adam and Eve, God states that the serpent would be defeated by one who is an "offspring of the woman," that is, he would be human. In the immediate context that woman was Eve (Gen 3:15).

In Genesis 17:6 God had promised to Abraham "kings shall come forth from you" and some of these kings would be through him and his wife Sarah who gave birth to Isaac (Gen 17:16). Later God repeated the promise to Isaac's son Jacob, "kings shall come forth from you" (Gen 35:11).

Up to this point in the biblical narrative, the promise was of many kings, but Jacob prophesied that one special ruler would emerge from the tribe of Judah, "The scepter shall not depart from Judah, nor the ruler's staff from between his feet, until Shiloh comes, and to him *shall be* the obedience of the peoples (Gen 49:10). The plural "peoples" hints that he will not just rule over the nation of Israel but also over all the Gentiles.

Several hundred years later, in the book of Numbers, Moses confirms that the Messiah would come from the nation of Israel. God makes this clear though the mouth of the false prophet Balaam just prior to Israel's entrance into Canaan, "I see him, but not now; I behold him, but not near: a star shall come out of Jacob, and a scepter shall rise out of Israel" (Num 24:17).

From the time of Moses to the implementation of the monarchy in Israel almost 400 years had passed. For that period charismatic leaders such as Moses and Joshua led the nation of Israel, and following them judges ruled. It was during the ministry of Samuel who served as a judge and a priest that the elders of Israel requested of him, "Appoint a king for us to judge us like all the nations" (1 Sam 8:5). The notion that God never wanted Israel to have a king for He alone was to be their ruler, is incorrect. It is true that God was in an ultimate sense their king (1 Sam 8:7), but as we have seen, not only did He promise that human kings would descend through Isaac, but He also gave detailed revelation in the Mosaic Law on how those kings were to act and live (Deut 17:14-20). Therefore, it was not the nation's request for a king in 1 Samuel 8 that was in error, but their desire to have a king that was "like all the nations" around them that was sinful (1 Sam 8:5). As a concession, God granted to them their first king, Saul who was a dismal failure because of his disobedience. God stated that Saul's kingdom would not endure, and the royal line would not descend through him (1 Sam 13:14; 15:26-28). Since Saul was from Benjamin, it was clear he was not in the messianic line which was to be through the tribe of Judah (Gen 49:10; Num 24:17).

It was with Saul's successor, David, who was from the tribe of Judah, that God made an eternal covenant (2 Sam 7:12-16; Ps 89). The promise made to David was that his line, or that One from his line would rule eternally on the throne. It was the prophet Isaiah that made it clear the Messiah would come from the family of Jesse (David's father),

Then a shoot will spring from the stem of Jesse, and a branch from his roots will bear fruit (Isa 11:1).

Further description by Isaiah makes clear he was speaking of the Messiah,

The Spirit of the LORD will rest on Him, the spirit of wisdom and understanding, the spirit of counsel and strength, the spirit of knowledge and the fear of the LORD. And He will delight in the fear of the LORD, and He will not judge by what His eyes see, nor make a decision by what His ears hear; but with righteousness He will judge the poor, and decide with fairness for the afflicted of the earth; and He will strike the earth with the rod of His mouth, and with the breath of His lips He will slay the wicked. Also righteousness will be the belt about His loins, and faithfulness the belt about His waist (Isa 11:2-5).

God's promise in 2 Samuel 7:12-16 made it clear that the promised King would emerge from the line of David. Solomon was the near fulfillment. But David understood the prophecy to refer to a distant king who would occupy an eternal throne, and rule over an eternal kingdom, "You have spoken also of the house of Your servant concerning the distant future" (2 Sam 7:16, 19). The authors of 1 and 2 Kings and 1 and 2 Chronicles traced the history of Israel's and Judah's kings. As we have seen, none of them turned out to be the Messiah and none of them ruled eternally on the throne of David.

The identity of the Messiah was further narrowed down by the prophet Micah. He prophesied that the messianic king would not only be a descendant of David, but he would more specifically be born in the little village of Bethlehem,

But as for you, Bethlehem Ephrathah, *too* little to be among the clans of Judah, from you One will go forth for Me to be ruler in Israel. His goings forth are from long ago, from the days of eternity (Mic 5:2).

We also note from this verse that the coming king will be eternal in nature, "His goings forth are...from the days of eternity." That creates a conundrum. How can the Messiah be both human and Divine as Micah 5:2 implies? Jesus himself confronted the religious rulers of his day with this same question in Matthew 22:45, "If David then calls Him 'Lord,' how is He his son?" In other words, if David refers to the Messiah as the Lord, how can he also be a human son born in the line of David?

The prophet Isaiah solves this dilemma in Isaiah 7:14 when prophesying to King Ahab, "Therefore, the Lord Himself will give you a sign: Behold, a virgin will be with child and bear a son, and she will call His name Immanuel." Immanuel means "God with us." The Messiah will be of a miraculous human birth, and the result will be that the child is called "God with us" alluding at his deity.

So, to summarize thus far in the prophetic record, the Messiah was to be of human origin, from the nation of Israel, of the tribe of Judah, from specific family of Jesse, through the line of David, born in the city of Bethlehem, and born of a virgin. All these specifications narrowed down the identity of the Messiah to but one possible individual.

CHAPTER 4

NEW TESTAMENT

KINGDOM

DEVELOPMENTS

ARRIVAL OF THE MESSIANIC KING

As mentioned above, none of the kings of the Old Testament period fulfilled God's promise that He would establish an eternal king who would rule over an eternal kingdom on the throne of David. With the Babylonian captivity, the monarchy in Israel in the line of David came to a bitter end. After the return from the captivity, though the line of David continued through Zerubbabel, the monarchy was not reestablished. For 400 years the Davidic line continued but without a king.

The Davidic line continued from Zerubbabel (after the captivity) right up to the time of Jesus (Matt 1:12-16; Luke 3:23-27). It is important to interpret the Gospels as the continuation of the Old Testament narrative; what God began and developed in the Old Testament, he carried on towards its climax and resolution in the New.

The book of Luke makes this connection between the Davidic kings and Jesus explicitly clear. It opens with an astonishing announcement from the angel Gabriel to the young virgin Mary,

> Behold, you will conceive in your womb and bear a son, and you shall name Him Jesus. He will be great and will be called the Son of the Most High; and the Lord God will give Him the throne of His father David; and He will reign over the house of Jacob forever, and His kingdom will have no end (Luke 1:31-33).

In their genealogies, both Luke and Matthew link Jesus directly to David, in the royal line of the promised Messiah (Matt 1:1-16; Luke 3:23-38).

It is of upmost importance to observe the connection between the original promised kingdom to David in 2 Samuel 7 and the identification of its ruler as Jesus in Luke 1, "the Lord God will give Him the throne *of His father David* (emphasis added); and He will reign over the house of Jacob forever" (Luke 1:32-33). It is this Davidic kingdom that Jesus refers to some thirty years later when he begins his ministry, "The time is fulfilled, and the kingdom of God is at hand" (Mark 1:15).

Let me return to our first and earliest prophecy from Genesis 3:15. We were promised the Messiah would be of the seed of a woman, a very strange statement since in procreation all human births are from the seed of a man, not a woman. There was only one birth in history that was of the seed of a woman, the virgin birth. According to the genealogies in Matthew 1 and Luke 3, Mary, not Joseph was the only one who contributed to Jesus' humanity.

Almost nine months after Mary conceived by the Holy Spirit (Matt 1:18; Luke 1:35) a census was required by Caesar Augustus, which required that Joseph and Mary to travel from where they were living to their tribal and family property which was in Bethlehem (Matt 2:1; Luke 2:4-7).

Thus, the Messiah did come exactly as predicted. He was a human as Genesis 3:15 promised, from the nation of Israel as pointed out in Numbers 24:17, from the tribe of Judah as stated in Genesis 49:10, from the family of Jesse (Isa 11:1), of the line of David (Luke 1:33), and born in the village of Bethlehem (Mic 5:2) through a virgin (Isa 7:14; Matt 1:23). God himself took on human flesh (John 1:1, 14).

THE FIRST ADVENT MINISTRY AND KINGDOM MESSAGE OF THE MESSIAH

There was great expectation for the arrival of the Messiah at the time of Christ's birth and at the beginning of his earthly ministry (Matt 2:4-5; 12:23; 22:42; Luke 2:38; John 1:19-20, 41, 45; 4:29). Many Jews at that time had been waiting for the reestablishment of the Davidic kingdom, believing the promised Messiah would do so (Luke 2:25-32; John 1:19-27). That was the only kingdom that they were aware of that had been promised in the prophets. Some thirty years after the birth of Jesus, John the Baptist appears on the scene to officially introduce the Messiah to the nation of Israel.

THE NECESSITY OF THE NATION'S REPENTANCE

Matthew reveals that John's message to the Jews was that they should repent,

> In those days John the Baptist came preaching in the wilderness of Judea, "Repent, for the kingdom of heaven is at hand" (Matt 3:2).

Mark confirms that John's message was repentance,

> John appeared, baptizing in the wilderness and proclaiming a baptism of repentance for the forgiveness of sins (Mark 1:4).

When Jesus started his public ministry, he continued John's call to repentance,

> From that time Jesus began to preach, saying, "Repent, for the kingdom of heaven is at hand" (Matt 4:17).

Mark records Jesus' message with similar words,

> The time is fulfilled, and the kingdom of God is at hand; repent and believe in the gospel (Mark 1:15).

The gospel at that time would not have been the good news of Christ's death and resurrection because those events had not yet taken place. Rather, the good news was that the Messiah had finally arrived, and the long-awaited "kingdom" promised to David (2 Sam 7:12-16) and announced by Isaiah (Isa 9:6-7) was at hand, that is, it was about to be established. In the mind of the first-century Jew, the kingdom that the Gospel writers presented to the nation, at least in the beginning of Synoptic Gospels, is clearly linked to the Davidic kingdom, a Davidic king reigning on the throne of David in the city of Jerusalem (Ps 2:6; Luke 1:31-32).

The Jews of that day would have naturally understood Jesus to be referring to the promised Davidic kingdom for which they had been waiting hundreds of years. Many readers today mistakenly read into that original kingdom message a contemporary idea of believing in Christ so that they may be assured of entering heaven. That concept does come later in God's revelation but is foreign to this historical context. They were thinking of a literal earthly kingdom, and the Gospel writers do not correct that notion.

When John the Baptist and Jesus the Messiah spoke of a kingdom that was at hand, they were not introducing a new concept of the kingdom but an old one, one that had been promised to David (Ps 89:3-4, 18, 20-29; 2 Sam 7:8-13, 16;

1 Chron 17:7-14) and predicted by the prophets (Isa 9:7; Dan 2:44; 7:14, 18, 22, 27; Obad 21; Micah 4:8).

Some argue that Matthew's "kingdom of heaven" and Mark's "kingdom of God" refer to two separate kingdom concepts, but the use of the phrases in the similar contexts suggests that they are synonymous or nearly so. The point that I would emphasize is that the initial message of both John the Baptist and Jesus was a call to repentance, because the kingdom promised in the Old Testament was about to be set up in Israel where it had been long awaited. This implies that one could not enter the Messiah's kingdom on earth without repenting. It is also clear that the kingdom of which Jesus speaks was at hand but had not yet come. In the Sermon on the Mount, Jesus teaches the disciples to pray, "Your kingdom come," implying it was still future and still yet to come at the time of Jesus' public ministry (Matt 6:10).

THE MESSIAH'S MIRACLES AND THE KINGDOM

The miracles that Jesus performed served several purposes but at least one of them was to demonstrate that he was the true Messiah (Mark 2:12; 4:41), and he had the power to bring in the promised kingdom. The miracles were, so to speak, his credentials as cited by Isaiah and confirmed by Matthew (cf. Isa 35:4-6; 61:1; Matt 11:2-5). Some may argue that the Jews entertained a faulty expectation of a kingdom, and Jesus was instead really offering them entrance into a merely spiritual kingdom. If that were the case, Jesus made no effort to correct their expectation that the kingdom was to be established in Israel, extend to the whole earth, and that the Messiah would rule from the throne of David. But he did insist that the nation would first have to repent before that kingdom would come. That was the one caveat. The establishment of the promised Davidic kingdom was contingent on the national repentance of Israel. This truth harmonizes with what the Old Testament prophets taught. At this point in God's unfolding revelation, that kingdom had not been directly promised to any particular nation except Israel, though several prophecies did state that Gentiles would also participate in it.

After his initial appearance to the nation, Jesus explained that it was necessary for him to preach the message of the kingdom of God in the cities of Israel (Luke 4:43). He sent out his apostles not to the Gentiles but to the Jews, for at that historical point they were the primary recipients to whom the kingdom had been promised,

> These twelve Jesus sent out after instructing them: "Do not go in *the* way of *the* Gentiles, and do not enter *any* city of the Samaritans; but rather go to the lost sheep of the house of Israel" (Matt 10:5-6).

The apostles preached, as John and Jesus before them, that all should repent, "They went out and preached that *men* should repent" (Mark 6:12).

Jesus also gave power to his twelve disciples to perform miraculous works, "Jesus summoned His twelve disciples and gave them authority over unclean spirits, to cast them out, and to heal every kind of disease and every kind of sickness" (Matt 10:1). At least one purpose of these miracles was that they offered evidence that Jesus whom they preached was the Messiah. So, the initial purpose of Christ ministry to Israel was to give proof that he was the awaited Messiah and to require repentance of the nation if they desired to enter the kingdom that was being offered. In fact, later, Jesus twice warns, "I tell you, no, but unless you repent, you will all likewise perish" (cf. Luke 13:3, 5).

It is crucial to see this link between the Old Testament promises of a coming Messiah and kingdom and the arrival of Jesus as that promised Messiah offering that promised kingdom to Israel. If this continuity between the Old Testament notion of the kingdom and that which Jesus offered to Israel is missed, then the interpreter is liable to see the kingdom that Jesus spoke about as something quite different from the prophetic picture given through the prophets.

It seems that often the default interpretation of many interpreters today is that Jesus was offering merely a spiritual kingdom. This calls into question the entire prophetic picture as laid out for thousands of years in the Old Testament and the Synoptic Gospels. It is not that the Old Testament writers described an unspiritual earthly kingdom, but rather an earthly kingdom that would be characterized by spiritual qualities (Matt 6:10).

I am not disputing that Jesus called individuals to faith in himself and to personal repentance for the forgiveness of their sins (Matt 9:6; 11:28-29; John 1:12; 3:3). When that happens, the believer enters the spiritual kingdom of God (Col 1:13). But what Jesus was offering to Israel in the opening chapters of the Synoptic Gospels was the promised Davidic kingdom. I am simply making a distinction. There is such a thing as faith in Christ and personal salvation, but there was also such a thing as the offer of the Davidic kingdom to Israel.

REJECTION OF THE MESSIAH AND HIS REQUIREMENT OF REPENTANCE

Jesus and his disciples were preaching the message that repentance was the condition for entering the kingdom that was yet to be established. But it quickly becomes apparent that that condition was not being met by the majority in the nation of Israel and particularly the religious leadership. In the healing of the ten lepers in Luke 17:11-19, only one came back to thank Jesus, and the comment that Jesus makes depicts the response of the Jews to their Messiah. In v. 18 Jesus says, "Was no one found who returned to give glory to God, except this foreigner?" After the miracle that Jesus had performed to heal these lepers, only one responded positively to him, and he was not even a Jew but a foreigner. Among the Jewish public, Jesus' message of repentance fell largely on deaf ears.

On the way to Jerusalem, prior to the passion week, Luke says that the disciples thought that the kingdom was about to appear (Luke 19:11). This means that at that point in the Messiah's ministry the kingdom had not yet come. The Pharisees then asked him "when the kingdom of God was coming" (Luke 17:20). Their question implied that if Jesus was truly the Messiah, then he would be establishing his kingdom as promised in the prophets, yet they were not seeing it. Jesus' answer is enlightening,

> "The kingdom of God is not coming with signs to be observed; nor will they say, 'Look, here *it is!*' or, 'There *it is!*' For behold, the kingdom of God is in your midst" (Luke 17:20-21).

Some have suggested that his answer is proof that Jesus never offered a literal physical kingdom but only spiritual one. Yet here in Luke 17 he was talking to the Pharisees, those who were rejecting him as Messiah. Surely, Jesus did not mean that they should look inside themselves to discover the kingdom of God for he had earlier said that inside they were full of "dead men's bones and all uncleanness" (Matt 23:27). More likely Jesus meant that the kingdom was right in their midst, right before their eyes in the person of the Messiah. He was the One who had the authority and power to bring in the kingdom and unless they repented, responded in faith, and embraced him as Messiah, they would not see that kingdom established in Israel. The kingdom was tied to their embracing the Messiah.

The Gospel writers make it clear that widespread repentance did not occur in Israel. As a result, Matthew records, "Then He began to denounce the cities in which most of His miracles were done, because they did not repent" (Matt 11:20). Let's remember that his miracles were his credentials giving clear evidence that he was indeed the promised Messiah. As a result of their rejection, in Luke 13:35 Jesus says, "Behold, your house is forsaken. And I tell you, you will not see me until you say, 'Blessed is he who comes in the name of the Lord!'" (a quote taken from Ps 118:26). Later, he goes on to say, "Therefore I say to you, the kingdom of God will be taken away from you and given to a people, producing the fruit of it" (Matthew 21:43).

As late as the passion week (the last week of Jesus' earthly life), after his triumphal entry into Jerusalem, he talks about the kingdom of God still lying in the future. In Matthew 24:3, his disciples ask him what signs would occur to signal his Second Coming. He mentioned a series of signs that would appear before the Second Advent, among them "signs in the sun, moon, and stars" (Luke 21:25). He also said, "This gospel of the kingdom shall be preached in the whole world as a testimony to all the nations, and then the end will come" (Matt 24:14), indicating that at that future time, just before the Second Coming, the promised Davidic kingdom was still viewed as future. By now it was clear that the nation had not repented, the kingdom that had been initially offered and preached had not been established, but it was still to come after future apocalyptic signs, "When you see these things [the signs] happening, recognize that the kingdom of God is near" (Luke 21:31).

By the time Christ sat down with his disciples at the last supper, it was clear that the Davidic kingdom had not been established but was still promised for a future day, "But I say to you, I will not drink of this fruit of the vine from now on until that day when I drink it new with you in My Father's kingdom" (Matt 26:29). We may be tempted here to interpret the kingdom in that verse as the kingdom in heaven, but the context is still the Davidic kingdom and drinking from the "fruit of the vine" implies an earthly setting. Jesus is telling his disciples that the promised Davidic kingdom is still going to come, and he will celebrate in it with them at that time.

After Jesus' death and resurrection, two disciples on the road to Emmaus who did not recognize Jesus when he appeared to them, unwittingly said to him, "We were hoping that it was He who was going to redeem Israel" (Luke 24:21). This implies that they believed that Jesus had failed to do so. Soon after that, his disciples asked him if at that time he was going to "restore the kingdom to Israel" (Acts 1:6). This means two things about the disciples' understanding. First, they understood that the kingdom had not been established at Christ's First Advent, and second, the kingdom to be established was a restored one, meaning it had existed previously. This no doubt refers to the Davidic kingdom that had been terminated at the Babylonian captivity in 586 BC but promised to return to Israel.

The promised restoration of the Davidic kingdom did not take place. Instead, Jesus was "the stone that the builders rejected" (Matt 21:42). As a response to this rejection of the Messiah and a failure of the nation to repent, the offer for the imminent establishment of the Davidic kingdom was withdrawn until a future time. It is not until Revelation 11:15, after the occurrence of many of the signs announced in the Olivet Discourse, that "The seventh angel will sound his trumpet, and loud voices in heaven will announce, 'The kingdom of the world has become the kingdom of our Lord and of his Christ, and He shall reign forever and ever.'" Even after the Second Coming of Christ to earth, at the judgment of the nations, Christ will surprise many who claim to have faith in him by saying he does not know them. Because of this, they will not enter the kingdom. It is at that point in time when the kingdom of God will be established on earth (Matt 7:21-23; 25:31-34, 41, 46).

Thus far, as we have traced the prediction and promise of a kingdom on earth, it begins to become more apparent that the content of the Bible, Old and New Testaments together, concerns itself with the revelation of God's purpose of reestablishing his rule over the earth.

CONTINGENCY IN GOD'S DEALINGS

God is indeed completely sovereign, yet that reality in no way excludes but rather includes (or incorporates) human response into his working. The establishment (or reestablishment) of the Davidic kingdom was contingent upon Israel's repentance. Contingency is not at odds with God's sovereignty but part and parcel of it. Contingency was always built into God's sovereign purpose of saving Israel. We have already seen that at the First Advent for God to establish the Davidic kingdom promised to David and his descendants, Israel had to repent, the nation had to believe Jesus was God's Messiah. If they did not, their kingdom would not be established. It is akin to the offer of salvation. God is truly sovereign in saving, but that does not negate human responsibility to repent and believe. It is not that human faith is a work that acquires salvation, but it is the vehicle through which it is received. Or take the example of God's *sovereign* will that on the divine level determines all things that come to pass and yet simultaneously on another level (his *permissive* will) charges us with the responsibility of responding to him. This is not double-speak but both levels of reality co-exist. So, it is a paradox but not a contradiction when we assert that God on the one hand is entirely sovereign over salvation and that the individual, on the other hand, determines whether he or she will accept that offer of salvation. It is true that God must grant repentance and yet He calls men to repent and expects them to respond (2 Tim 2:25). When they don't, they are held responsible for their refusal.

In the case of Israel, there was a genuine offer of the kingdom, yet there had to also be repentance, and the Messiah had to be accepted by the nation (Matt 3;2; 4:17). At that point in history, God's covenant people resisted and rejected his claims, eventually committing blasphemy in their rejection by attributing Christ's miracles, which were his messianic credentials, to the work of Satan (Matt 12:31). As a result, the Davidic kingdom was never established but rather withheld until the nation would say, "Blessed is He who comes in the name of the Lord" (Matt 23:39). In other words, the kingdom would not be established until the nation repented and accepted her Messiah.

Since the Messiah was spurned, the offer of that promised kingdom was rescinded, albeit temporarily (Rom 11:25), until the nation would respond to the Messiah's call to repent. After Pentecost, the Apostle Peter told the Jews that the condition for the Messiah's return (apart from God's sovereign timing), was their repentance,

> Therefore repent and return, so that your sins may be wiped away, in order that times of refreshing may come from the presence of the Lord; and that He may send Jesus, the Christ appointed for you, whom heaven must receive until *the* period of restoration of all things about which God spoke by the mouth of His holy prophets from ancient time (Acts 3:19-21).

In other words, the Messiah would remain in heaven at God's right hand until the nation repented and accepted Jesus as its Messiah. Then he would return to bring about the promised restoration.

In light of Israel's rejection of Christ, Jesus warned in the parable of the vineyard that they would lose their right to be stewards of the land of Israel. In fact, God would bring judgment on the nation, "He will bring those wretches to a wretched end, and will rent out the vineyard to other vine-growers who will pay him the proceeds at the *proper* seasons" (Matt 21:41). Similarly, Jesus said, "Therefore I say to you, the kingdom of God will be taken away from you and given to a people, producing the fruit of it" (Matt 21:43). The term used for "people" is *ethnos* (singular), so one people group is meant. Some argue that this could not refer to the church because the church is not a single people group but is made up of many peoples. However, 1 Peter 2:9 and possibly Romans 10:19 refer to the church as a single people group (albeit from many nations). But even if Jesus was referring to the church, he is not saying that the kingdom promised to David will be established in the church. Rather the kingdom promised to David will be put on hold and a new form of the kingdom will be manifested in the church (which I explain in the following chapter). But even if Jesus was referring to the church, and I'm not convinced he was, it does not necessarily follow that the church has replaced Israel forever. There is another plausible interpretation of Matthew 21:43. Jesus may be simply promising the kingdom to a future "people" that is a future generation of Jews who will "produce the "fruit of it," that is they will come to faith in him as their Messiah.

This view harmonizes with other prophetic statements that indicate at some point in God's sovereign plan, God will pour out his Spirit on the nation of Israel and multitudes of them will come to faith in their Messiah (Isa 60; Ezek 36–37; Zech 12:10–13:1). Thus, God will providentially decide to show mercy, and that mercy will draw multitude of Jews from all over the world to their Messiah, they will repent and believe. That generation will produce the fruit of the kingdom.

CHAPTER 5

MYSTERIES OF THE KINGDOM

Naturally, the question arises; if Jesus is the true Messiah and he did genuinely offer the kingdom that had been promised by the Old Testament prophets, but the nation rejected him, then what happens to the kingdom after his rejection, death, and resurrection?

In response to the national widespread rejection of the Messiah, Jesus taught that the Davidic kingdom would not be established at his First Advent. Rather, it would come at a future time when the Jewish nation repented and welcomed him as their true Messiah, "Behold, your house is left to you *desolate*; and I say to you, you will not see Me until *the time* comes when you say, 'Blessed is he who comes in the name of the Lord!'" (Luke 13:35).

In the meantime, the kingdom work of God in the present age would take on new form. In Matthew 13:11, Mark 4:11, and Luke 8:10 Jesus referred to the "mysteries" of the kingdom. These mysteries signal new revelations about the kingdom in light of Israel's rejection of the Messiah. These new truths were not taught in the Old Testament but had now come to light in view of the nation's rejection of the Davidic king. These mysteries reveal several things about the kingdom in the present age that were not known in the Old Testament era. Matthew says they were "things hidden from the foundation of the world" (Matt 13:35). They reveal what would happen in relation to the advancement of God's kingdom in the present age in light of the nation's rejection of their Messiah.

THE KINGDOM PARABLES

New or mystery kingdom truths were given in the form of parables. The reason for this is that parables served the dual purpose of revealing new truth to those who were responding in faith to the Messiah (13:11-12, 16-17, 52) while at the same time hiding these truths from those who were rejecting him (13:11b, 13-15). Hiding truth from those rejecting the Messiah was a form of judgment on their willful unbelief and rejection (Isa 6:10; Matt 13:14-15).

The kingdom parables chronicle the spiritual progress of God's kingdom in the present age, beginning with the propagation of the kingdom message (the parable of the sower) and ending with the second coming and establishment of the millennial (Davidic) kingdom (the parable of the dragnet).

Matthew 13:52 reveals that these parables teach both old and new truths. Jesus says that every scribe who is a disciple of the kingdom brings both "new" and "old" things out of his treasure. This means that in these parables there are old truths carried over from the Old Testament revelation about the kingdom, and there are new truths that were not revealed in the Old Testament. These new truths now come to light in view of Israel's rejection of her Messiah. The parables in question are most extensively revealed in Matthew 13 but also in Mark 4 and in Luke 8:4-18; 13:18-21.

1. *The parable of the sower* (**Matt 13:3-9, 18-23**). In this parable a sower distributes seed that falls on various soils. Notice that the seed is the "word of the kingdom" not the message about the death and resurrection of the Messiah. The soil produces various responses illustrating the differing responses to the kingdom message by Israel (13:1-9, 18-23). The view of the kingdom in the Old Testament was that God would suddenly intervene with great power to establish it on the earth, and the Jews felt they would all automatically be part of it since they were descendants of Abraham (cf. Daniel 2:44; 7:27; Luke 3:8; John 8:33). But the parable of the sower revealed that the message of the Messiah's kingdom, the "seed" sown, would not be accepted by the majority of those who heard it, in fact it would be rejected by most, for various reasons. This new reality was never foreseen in the Old Testament's view of the coming kingdom but was now part of the truth in this age.

2. *Parable of the growing seed* (**Mark 4:26-29**). In this parable (found only in Mark) a man cast seed upon the soil and with time it grows. The parable teaches that in this age the kingdom would mysteriously grow, but that growth would not be immediately visible to the human eye. What was new in this teaching was that the kingdom in the present age would not come suddenly with dramatic visible power as portrayed by the Old Testament prophets, but rather by an invisible or internal power, and its spread would involve a gradual process akin to the growth of a plant.

3. *The parable of the tares* (**Matt 13:24-30, 36-43**). In this parable, good seed is sown but an enemy sows bad seed alongside of it. They grow together until the end of the age when they are separated. The bad seed goes into judgment and the good seed into God's kingdom. The parable reveals Satan's

work of opposing the message of the Messiah. It results in believers and non-believers coexisting in the present world. In this parable, the" field" is not the church but the "world." The newly revealed truth in the parable is the idea that in the present age both wheat and tares, believers and non-believers, coexist. The tares would not be removed until the Second Coming of Messiah in power and glory. This concept is new because Israel expected the Messiah to eradicate all opponents when he set up His kingdom. All unbelievers would be judged, and the kingdom would begin only with believers on the earth. But that will not be true until the Second Coming. Also, this parable teaches that there would be a delay before the judgment comes at the end of this age.

4. *The parable of the mustard seed* (Matt 13:31-32). In this parable a tiny mustard seed is sown, but it eventually grows into a plant so large so that even birds can nest in its branches. The parable revealed that in this present age the kingdom will start out tiny in size. But there would be significant growth over time. Its final size will contrast greatly with its beginning size. The birds nesting in its branches may imply that even those not directly a part of the kingdom will nevertheless enjoy or take advantage of its influence in this age, or it may mean that the kingdom will simply be a source of protection and rest. New was the concept that it would begin small and slowly grow, rather than suddenly engulf the whole earth as the Old Testament had portrayed. It would begin with a small group of Jews, the disciples, but then gradually spread to all nations.

5. *The parable of the leaven* (Matt 13:33). In this parable the kingdom of God is compared to leaven hidden in a piece of dough that works invisibly and slowly to eventually leaven the whole piece of dough. Since leaven in the Bible almost always signifies evil, some expositors hold that this parable reveals that there will be an expanding growth of evil in the present age, contemporaneous with the growth of the kingdom. Or it may simply reveal that the kingdom's growth in this age will be almost imperceptible yet continual. The new revelation is that the kingdom will expand slowly in contrast to the Old Testament belief that it would break in upon the world suddenly with supernatural force. If leaven signifies evil, then this parable also teaches that evil will continue to be present in this age of the kingdom in a way that was not expected by Old Testament prophets.

6. *The parable of the hidden treasure* **(Matt 13:44).** In this parabolic comparison Jesus says the kingdom of God is like a hidden treasure which when found causes a person to sell all they have to buy the field in which the treasure is hidden. This emphasizes the priceless value of the kingdom and the joy it brings to the person who discovers or finds it. In contrast to the promised Davidic kingdom, its presence is not seen in an external glorious form, but rather it appears hidden from the human eye. But once it is found, its value supersedes all earthly value. New is the idea that it is hidden (or invisible) and was seemingly found by chance.

7. *The parable of the pearl of great price* **(Matt 13:45).** The kingdom is compared to a merchant seeking fine pearls in this parable. When he finds one, he sells all he has to obtain it. This comparison is similar to the previous one, except in this case the one finding the kingdom has to search diligently to find it. As in the previous parable, this one teaches that the kingdom itself is of such a supreme value, that the one discovering it would gladly give up all wealth or earthly possessions to have it (some expositors interpret the one searching as the Messiah, who valued it so much that he gave up his own life to purchase it). New is the idea that the kingdom in

49

this age is not externally observable as Old Testament saints expected it to be, rather one must search diligently to find it.

8. *The parable of the dragnet* (Matt 13:47-50). In this parable the kingdom of God in this age is compared to a dragnet that was cast into the sea and gathered both good and bad fish. Once the net was brought to shore, the bad fish were disposed of and the good fish kept. This parable revealed that the judgment of God will not separate the true and false believers until the end of the age; at that time all the wicked will be judged and righteous will enter the kingdom (13:47-50). New is the idea that the kingdom in this age would consist of a mixture of good and bad people and not until the end would they be separated, and not till the end would the Messiah's kingdom on earth be established.

9. *The parable of the householder* (Matt 13:52). In this final comparison, Jesus says that a scribe who is a disciple of the kingdom is like the head of a household who has a treasure, and out of this treasure he brings both old and new things. This verse is key to understanding what Jesus is doing with these parables. He is teaching that some features of the new or mystery form of the kingdom are identical to features previously revealed about the millennial kingdom in the Old Testament, but other features are entirely new. Jesus is revealing both the old features and the new.

What these parables reveal about the advancement of God's kingdom is that even though the literal Davidic kingdom was not established at the First Advent, a mystery form or new form of the kingdom is advancing in this age. It has some characteristics similar to those taught in the Old Testament about the kingdom, but it also has some entirely new features that heretofore had not been revealed. The Davidic kingdom will come at the end of the age.

THE CHURCH IN GOD'S KINGDOM PROGRAM

As the nation of Israel made clear that it was rejecting Jesus as the Messiah, Christ began to reveal his new purpose by announcing, "I will build My church" (Matt 16:18). Israel's rejection of Christ came to a climax when her leaders requested of the Romans that he be crucified. In this we see God's sovereign plan. He planned for the death and resurrection of the Messiah to be the very means by which He would forgive sins and thus provide for the salvation of his future church (John 1:12-13; Rom 3:23-26).

Since we occupy the historical period of the church, we tend to think it is the apex of God's purpose. The church does have the special place in Christ's heart (Eph 5:25, 29, 32), but when we consider the entire biblical revelation, we see that the church comprises just one of God's great purposes. This book is not focused on the church per se, but on the wider purposes of God, and in particular the establishing of his kingdom on the earth. The church is one major part of God's kingdom program.

In Matthew 16:18 when Jesus prophesied the building of the church, it was still future, "I will build My church." Acts 2 records the pouring out of the Spirit and the birth of the church. The following chapters in Acts chronicle its growth during its infancy. This was a new work of God that began at Pentecost and will end its earthly sojourn when Christ comes for his church (cf. Acts 2:1-4; John 14:2-3; 1 Cor 15:50-55; 1 Thess 4:13-18).

Though the Old Testament prophets did foresee a time when Gentile nations would stream to Israel, the specific revelation of the church made up of both Jews and Gentiles unified in one spiritual body, having equal access to God lay hidden in the counsel of God first to be revealed by Jesus when he said, "I will build my church" (Matt 16:18).

It was to the Apostle Paul that God gave divine revelation about the unique nature of the church. It consists of both Jews

51

and Gentiles having equal access to God (Eph 2:18; 3:12; Heb 4:16), something that was not true under the Law. In the church, every member is baptized into the body of Christ, through a spiritual baptism that did not exist before the pouring out of the Spirit at Pentecost (Acts 2:1-4; 1 Cor 12:13). Another significant feature of the church is that each member is indwelt eternally by the Holy Spirit in contrast to the temporal empowering during the time of the Old Testament. For example, when King Saul sinned, the Spirit departed from him, but for the believer today the Spirit will never leave the believer (cf. 1 Sam 16:13-14; John 14:17; Rom 8:9; Heb 13:5). Because of the unique and new work of the Spirit in the life of the believer in the body of Christ, there naturally results an intimate relationship between the Lord and each believer.

One of Christ's many purposes with believers in the church is to prepare them to become royal priests who will rule with him (1 Pet 2:5, 9; Rev 1:6). In Matthew 19:28, Jesus told his disciples that they would judge the twelve tribes of Israel, and in Revelation 20:4 those resurrected are promised that they will reign with him. God had "purchased men from every tribe and tongue and people and nation" so that they would serve him as priests and "reign upon the earth" (Rev 5:9-10). The Apostle Paul also believed in this reality. In correcting the Corinthians who thought they had already become kings, he said "I wish that you had become kings so that we also might reign with you" (1 Cor 4:8). Paul understood there was a future reign coming for believers. In the Apostle John's letter to the church at Thyratira, Jesus promises a future reign to believers,

> He who overcomes, and he who keeps My deeds until the end, to him I will give authority over the nations; and he shall rule them with a rod of iron, as the vessels of the potter are broken to pieces, as I also have received *authority* from My Father (Rev 2:26-27).

52

Also, to the church of Laodicea Jesus promises, "He who overcomes, I will grant to him to sit down with Me on My throne, as I also overcame and sat down with My Father on His throne" (Rev 3:21). Notice that Christ distinguishes here between his throne and his Father's throne. He sits on his Father's throne now in heaven (Heb 1:3). But at his second coming after returning to earth, he will sit on the throne of David, "But when the Son of Man comes in His glory, and all the angels with Him, then He will sit on His glorious throne" which Isaiah identifies as "the throne of David and his kingdom" (cf. Isa 9:7; Matt 25:31).

To summarize this point, God used the rejection of the Davidic kingdom by Israel to result in the death and resurrection of the Messiah, through whom he would redeem and prepare a kingdom of priests who could one day populate the kingdom on earth and co-rule with him.

If the apostles and the church are destined to co-rule with Christ in the coming kingdom on the earth, then this presupposes that they must be resurrected to do so. This means that believers in their resurrected bodies will co-mingle with those entering the millennial kingdom in their natural bodies. This has seemed improbable to some interpreters and has been one of arguments leveled against the notion of a millennial rule on the earth. Yet Christ in his resurrected body has already given us the precedent for such a condition. He was in his resurrected body while co-mingling with his disciples in their natural bodies and this was not thought to be impossible. Their interaction with one another was normal.

Though the kingdom envisioned by the Old Testament prophets was not established during the First Advent, Christ nevertheless continued to prepare for the day when the nation would repent and the kingdom would come in its fullness and glory.

CHAPTER 6

FREQUENT OBJECTIONS TO THE MILLENNIUM

Some ask, why is debate about the millennium even important? We are part of the church, we all love Jesus, we know where we are going, so what difference does it make if there is a millennium or not? What benefit is there in even discussing such matters? Let me refer to a seminal statement made by Moses. As the nation of Israel was about to enter the Promise Land, he reminded them, "The secret things belong to the LORD our God, but the things revealed belong to us and to our sons forever, that we may observe all the words of this law" (Deut 29:29). If God thinks it is important enough to reveal to us his purposes in the Bible and give us insight to his plans that unfold and are revealed to us over thousands of years, then he must believe that these revelations are important for our life of faith. He knows what we need to know and what he wants us to know. Jesus said to his disciples, "I have called you friends, for all things that I have heard from My Father I have made known to you" (John 15:15). Also, knowledge of God's word is designed for our joy, "These things I have spoken to you so that My joy may be in you, and *that* your joy may be made full" (John 15:11). Our knowledge of these things and our expectation for their fulfillment will not only be instrumental in producing holiness in our lives (1 Pet 3:14) but will also increase our joy and hope, and ultimately contribute to our desire to praise God for His amazing plans. Therefore, I don't believe that the discussion of future things of which God has taken great pains to reveal to us is unimportant.

DID THE CHURCH REPLACE ISRAEL?

Since AD 70 when the Romans destroyed the temple in Jerusalem, murdered multitudes of Jews, and drove the rest out of the city into the diaspora, many Christian theologians have believed that God was through with the nation of Israel. Their rejection of their Messiah was the straw that broke the camel's back. The argument runs, God began a new people, the church and the church became the new Israel. It is true that God began a new spiritual work of building the church, but is the church the new Israel? I would agree with the thought that the church is now God's primary witness to the nations and the nation of Israel is not. But I also believe that the Scripture teaches that God will one day return to his work with the nation of Israel as the olive tree illustration in Romans 11:23-24 and many prophecies indicate. God is able to graft Israel back into his sovereign elective purposes.

Jesus did say the kingdom would be taken from Israel and given to a people, literally "a nation," who would produce its fruit (Matt 21:43). Peter identified the church as a "holy nation," a term that once applied to Israel (Exod 19:1-7). Many also argue that Paul believed that the church was the new Israel in God's plan (cf. Rom 2:28-29; 9-6-7; Gal 6:16). Has the church then replaced Israel? I want to qualify my answer. I don't believe that the church is the new Israel. The church is the church, and Israel is Israel. I would, however, agree that the church has replaced Israel for the present time as God's primary witness to the world. But this doesn't mean that the church has replaced Israel forever as God's witness on the earth, nor does it mean that the church is Israel.

Distinguishing the church from Israel is important. Israel is an ethnic people group descended from Abraham through Isaac. By way of contrast, the church is a group comprised of all nations, all ethnic groups, Jews and Gentiles indwelt by Christ and united to him by the Spirit (1 Cor 12:13; Eph 2:11-22; Col 1:27). If the church has replaced Israel, then there is no need for a literal fulfillment of the covenants and kingdom promised in the Old Testament. If the church fulfills those covenants or if the new heaven and earth fulfill those promises, we need look no further for them to find a future fulfillment in a millennium. But I would argue that Scripture repeatedly identifies the physical descendants of Abraham as Israel and the spiritual descendants of Abraham, believers after Pentecost (both Jews and Gentiles), as the church. In the case of believing Jews, they are both physical and spiritual descendants of Abraham. We can only conflate Israel with the church by employing an allegorical method of interpretation to make passages speaking about Israel in the Old Testament to refer to the church in the New. However, in their contexts most of these passages call for a literal interpretation. This does not deny that some prophetic passages have typical, symbolic, poetic, or apocalyptic features, but nevertheless have a literal rather than allegorical referent. In other words, when the Scripture speaks of Israel, the descendants of Abraham through Isaac and Jacob are meant.

For much of church history, Christians have held that the death of the Messiah in the Gospels and the beginning of the church in the Book of Acts followed by the Roman invasion of

Palestine in AD 66–70 marked the end of the Jewish nation. It was held that the church had replaced Israel as God's people (I do not disagree that the church makes up the people of God today, but it does not automatically follow that it has replaced Israel). Along with this history, several New Testament passages have been appealed to, to support this view. The primary passages that come into question are Romans 2:28-29; 9:6-7, and Galatians 6:15-16.

In Romans 2:28-29 Paul argues that a true Jew is not one who is merely circumcised in the flesh, that is, one who is merely a physical descendant of Abraham, but true Jews are those physical descendants of Abraham who have also experienced spiritual circumcision of the heart.

> For he is not a Jew who is one outwardly, nor is circumcision that which is outward in the flesh. But he is a Jew who is one inwardly; and circumcision is that which is of the heart, by the Spirit, not by the letter; and his praise is not from men, but from God.

This seems clear enough, but some interpreters have maintained that *all* those who have experienced heart circumcision are the true Jews. According to this logic, since the church consists of those people who are circumcised in their hearts, they make up the true Jews. But this interpretation misses Paul's point. Paul is not saying that the Gentiles and Jews who have a circumcised heart (have been born again) make up a new Israel. He is simply pointing out that there is a difference between Jews who have experienced the new birth (circumcision of the heart) and Jews who have not. His point is that those Jews who have experienced the circumcision of the heart, like Paul, have the Spirit and thus today are part of the church, but those Jews who do not have the Spirit are not part of the church. Thus, this passage does not argue that the church has replaced Israel. Rather it teaches that not all ethnic Jews are regenerated (circumcised of the heart) Jews.

In Romans 9:6-7 Paul puts forth similar argument. He says,

> They are not all Israel who are *descended* from Israel; nor are they all children because they are Abraham's descendants, but: "Through Isaac your descendants will be named."

Abraham had several children, Ishmael and Isaac, and later other children through Keturah (Gen 25:1). These were all physical descendants of Abraham. But the "promise" God made to bless (provide salvation through the Messiah) was to descend through just one of those children, Isaac. His point here is one of comparison. Just as all of Abraham's physical descendants were not of the promised line, so too not all Jews are believing Jews. In fact, most were not. Later we shall see that other prophesies make clear that God will not establish the kingdom promised to David with an unbelieving Jewish nation, but rather with one that will believe in the Messiah.

Galatians 6:15-16 is another passage that is often appealed to in order to claim that the church is the new Israel:

> For neither is circumcision anything, nor uncircumcision, but a new creation. And those who will walk by this rule, peace and mercy *be* upon them, and upon the Israel of God.

Paul's main point here is that in the era of the church it does not matter whether a person is physically circumcised or not, but what matters is that one has experienced the new birth. This of course applies to both Jew and Gentile. Then he concludes the thought by saying those who follow this teaching, "peace and mercy be upon them, and upon the Israel of God." Some interpreters have taken the "them" and the "Israel of God" to refer to the same group rather than two distinct groups. They translate the phrase in the following way, "peace and mercy be upon them, *even* the Israel of God" (emphasis mine) Thus, in this view the pronoun "them" is equated with the "Israel of God." In this interpretation they are both one and the same. They translate the Greek word *kai* as "even" making the two groups the same. Granted, *kai* can be translated as "even" but that is the rare exception. Normally, the conjunction *kai* is translated as "and." The repetition of the preposition "upon" in Galatians 6:16 signals that two distinct groups are meant rather than one,

> "Grace and mercy be *upon* them,
> and *upon* the Israel of God (emphasis added).

Paul is taking about two groups; one group consists of those Gentile believers who are adhering to Paul's teaching which he designates as "them," and the other group consists of those Jewish believers ("the Israel of God") who are also following Paul's teaching. So, the "Israel of God" here is not all believers (Jews and Gentiles, i.e., the church), but rather the Jewish believers within the church. The context of Galatians is that certain Jews, called Judaizers, were telling these Gentile believers that they had to be physically circumcised to be saved, that is, they had to keep the Law (Gal 2:15-16; 3:2). In contrast to those Jews, there were Jews among them who were genuine believers. They are the "Israel of God." But even if one were to grant the view that the "Israel of God" here refers to the whole church, which I don't, that still would not mean that God has reneged on his promises to the descendants of Abraham.

Throughout the book of Acts both Israel and the church remain side by side as two distinct groups and never is Israel called the church nor the church called Israel. Israel referred to ethnic Jews, and the church referred originally to believing Jews because they were the original believers that comprised the church. But later, once Gentiles began believing the gospel, the term church refers to both believing Jews and Gentiles. The term Israel occurs nineteen times in Acts and always refers to ethnic Israel. The term church occurs seventeen times. The first six of those occurrences are in Acts 5–11 when the church is still made up of primarily Jewish converts, and yet it remains distinct from Israel which is mentioned seven times in those same chapters. My point is that Israel and the church are distinct. They always have been. The Holy Spirit who inspired the Scriptures does not conflate the two.

THE KINGDOM AND THE CHURCH

Much the same can be said for the distinction between kingdom of God and the church. The church is one part or aspect of God's kingdom, but it is not exactly the same thing, for the kingdom is much more expansive.

For example, the kingdom of God can refer to God's sovereign rule over the entire universe, nothing excluded, "The LORD has established His throne in the heavens, and His sovereignty rules over all" (Ps 103:19). The writer of Chronicles says it this way, "Yours, O LORD, is the greatness and the power and the glory and the victory and the majesty, indeed everything that is in the heavens and the earth; Yours is the dominion, O LORD, and You exalt Yourself as head over all (1 Chron 29:11). The prophet Daniel confirms this claim, "His dominion is an everlasting dominion, and His kingdom *endures* from generation to generation" (cf. Ps 145:13; Dan 4:34). This all-encompassing idea of the kingdom includes all things and all events, "The One forming light and creating darkness, causing well-being and creating calamity; I am the LORD who does all these" (Isa 45:7). The prophet Amos states it this way, "If a trumpet is blown in a city will not the people tremble? If a calamity occurs in a city has not the LORD done it?" (Amos 3:6). This concept of God's sovereign kingdom has no condition for entrance, rather all men and all things are under its rule.

By way of contrast, God's theocratic kingdom on earth, as established in Israel in the Old Testament, was one historical manifestation of God's rule in the nation of Israel. Although it was part of God's sovereign rule, it did not include the Gentile nations as his sovereign rule over all things does. Later, the kingdom that Jesus offered had certain conditions for entrance, such as repentance. Not everyone and everything was part of it. It was to be a specific manifestation of God's rule on the earth.

The mystery kingdom that encompasses our present age is another manifestation of the kingdom (Matt 13). It is not the same as God's sovereign kingdom over all things, nor is it the same as his theocratic rule in Israel during much of the nation's history, nor is it to be equated with the coming kingdom to earth, "Your kingdom come." (Matt 6:10). The fact that the kingdom mentioned in Matthew 6:10 still needs to "come" makes clear that it is not the same as God's universal sovereign rule over all things for that universal kingdom has always existed, nor can it be the kingdom that now exists in the church for that kingdom is already come; but rather it refers to a future manifestation of God's rule on the earth, "Your kingdom come...on earth as it is in heaven" (Matt 6:10).

All of these are various expressions and aspects of God's kingdom. The point is that the coming millennial kingdom will be yet another phase or manifestation of God's kingdom on earth, but it is not the same as the church or his sovereign rule over all things, though it may share some those characteristics.

To summarize this section, it is a hermeneutical mistake to project the millennial passages either onto the church or the new heaven and earth. There is a church, and there is a new heaven and earth, but there is also a millennium. All of these are distinct and have their place in God's plan. Just as it would cause great confusion if we interpreted the Scriptures about the new heaven and earth as if they were describing the current church, so too would it cause bewilderment if we assigned Scriptures on the millennium to either the church or the new heaven and earth. We need to let the writers of Scripture say and describe with their words what they desire to depict, otherwise we run the danger of confusing ourselves and others and missing what God is saying.

IS GOD FINISHED WITH ISRAEL AS A NATION?

The Davidic kingdom offered to the Jewish nation at the beginning of the Synoptic Gospels was not a general call for all people to believe in Jesus so that they could go to heaven when they die. Christ had not yet died and was not yet resurrected. Rather, it was a specific offer of the promised Davidic kingdom. That offer was eventually rescinded because the nation had rejected Jesus as the legitimate Messiah. In light of that, Christ established his church which became a new manifestation of God's kingdom work in this present age. This has led some (or many) to argue that we should not expect God to fulfill his ancient promises to Israel in a literal manner; this includes his promise of an eternal king sitting on the throne of David in Jerusalem.

However, in Romans 11:23 Paul reminds us that God has the right and ability to graft Israel back into his salvation purposes. In Romans 11:25, Paul explains,

> For I do not want you, brethren, to be uninformed of this mystery—so that you will not be wise in your own estimation—that a partial hardening has happened to Israel *until the fullness of the Gentiles has come in* (emphasis mine).

God has temporarily put his plan for Israel on hold and is today building his church (Matt 16:18). When individual Jews, such as Paul, come to believe in Jesus as the Messiah, they become part of the body of Christ, the church (1 Cor 12:13). But at some point, the "fullness of the Gentiles" will be reached and those of the church, both living and dead, will be "caught up together...to meet the Lord in the air, and so we shall always be with the Lord" (1 Thess 4:17).

63

It is perhaps at that time that God will return to his plan to fulfill his purposes with the nation of Israel, "And so all Israel will be saved; just as it is written, the Deliverer will come from Zion, He will remove ungodliness from Jacob. This is my covenant with them when I take away their sins" (Rom 11:26-27). Paul is referring here to the New Covenant that Jesus procured (Luke 22:20) and Jeremiah had first proclaimed (Jer 31:31). But Israel's sins have not yet been forgiven for they have not yet entered into this covenant. They will not do so until they recognize Jesus as their Messiah.

A RETURN TO ANIMAL SACRIFICES?

Perhaps the most serious objection to a millennial reign is that advocates claim that a Jewish temple and its sacrificial system will be reinstituted in which animal sacrifices will once again be offered at a temple in Jerusalem. Millennialists assert that the nations will come to Israel and its rebuilt millennial temple to take part in the sacrificial system and the worship of God. Some even maintain that there will be a reinstituted priesthood from the line of Levi, descendants of Zadok. They hold that Jews converted to their Messiah will offer animal sacrifices (bulls, rams, goats, and lambs, burnt offerings, peace offerings, sin offerings, guilt offerings, and grain and meal offerings). They will keep the Sabbath and celebrate the Feast of Booths. Passages from several prophets are appealed to, in order to make this argument (cf. Isa 19:21; 56:7; Jer 33:18; Ezek 40; 38-42; 43:24; 44:11; 45:15, 23; 46:2, 4, 12; Zech 14:16-19, 21). Such a reversion to Mosaic-like practices is repulsive to many theologians.

Objectors to this millennial view point out that the writer of Hebrews teaches that the sacrifice of Christ was the culmination and completion of the sacrificial system. Jesus' sacrifice was "once for all," and that there is "no longer any need for an offering for sin" (Heb 9:25-26; 10:10,18). The Mosaic sacrificial system pointed to Christ's final sacrifice but never procured final atonement, "For it is impossible for the blood of bulls and goats to take away sins" (Heb 10:22). At best, returning to animal sacrifices is spiritually retroactive, at worse blasphemous, because they see it as a rejection of Christ's perfect and final sacrifice. What possible purpose could animal sacrifices serve in a future millennium?

A few observations may be helpful here. Even after the completion of Christ's perfect sacrifice for our sins and the sending of the Holy Spirit at Pentecost, some believers, even the Apostle Paul himself, offered animal sacrifices at the temple (Acts 21:26). This in no way spurned the sacrifice of Christ. It was not blasphemy. The argument of the apostles in Acts 15 was not that the Jews should no longer follow the Law, but that the Jews should not require believing Gentiles to keep the Law in order to be justified. No man (Gentile or Jew) could ever be justified before God by keeping the Law because no one can perfectly keep it, with the exception of Jesus. Justification could only come through faith in Christ, as Paul also plainly taught (Acts 15:11; Rom 2:14; Gal 2:16; Phil 3:1-7). In fact, many Jews who came to faith in Jesus as the Messiah (including Paul [Acts 21:20-26]) continued to keep the Mosaic Law, even offering animal sacrifices. They were not chastised for keeping the Law, making an animal sacrifice, nor prohibited from doing so. In fact, Paul was described positively as one who keeps the Law (Acts 21:24). So, the offering of animal sacrifices after the death of Christ would not necessarily be retroactive or insulting to God, depending on the purpose of those sacrifices.

A RETURN TO TEMPLE WORSHIP?

Why a temple? The Samaritan woman made clear that the Jews of that day thought worship was to take place at the temple in Jerusalem, but the Samaritans believed it should take place at their temple on mount Gerizim. Jesus replied that a time was coming "and now is" when God would be worshiped not in Jerusalem nor on Mt Gerizim but in "spirit and truth" (John 4:21-24). So, if that time has arrived as Jesus said it had, and believers today worship in "spirit and truth," what possible point could be served by having worship revert to a temple?

It is true that Jesus had told the Samaritan woman that a time was coming "and now is" that a person did not have to be in Jerusalem (where the temple was), or in any temple to worship God (John 4:21-24). Yet after the resurrection and sending of the Spirit, the apostles and other believers met in the temple daily (Acts 2:46). John and Peter went to the temple to pray (Acts 3:1), and as we have seen Paul went to the temple to offer sacrifices (Acts 21:20-26). The culminating sacrifice of Christ did take care of our sin once and forever, but it did not terminate the temple or temple worship by at least some of the apostles. It was the destruction of the Jerusalem temple by the Romans in AD 70 that made it no longer possible to worship there. Jesus' point in John 4:21-24 was not that a person should not worship in the temple, but that worship was not limited to the temple. Under Mosaic Law, God was to be approached through the priesthood and animal sacrifice. But after Pentecost every believer has "access" to God through the Spirit (Eph 2:18; 3:12). Access to God in the Spirit may be in a temple or outside of one. So, the rebuilding of a millennial temple does not conflict with the idea that God can be worshiped anywhere as long as it is in spirit and truth.

There is abundant revelation that clearly points to a millennial temple in Jerusalem. God's word must be the final arbiter in this matter. No matter how distasteful the idea of centralized worship with a temple in Jerusalem and animal sacrifices might be to the modern mind, the ultimate question is, does God's word reveal it to be the case? If so, we may perhaps then ask the question of why He might want to restore temple worship. But the same question may be posed regarding the millennium in general, why would God institute a millennial era that reveals a great advancement in every area of life both spiritual and physical yet falls short of the perfections of the eternal state? Why not just move directly into the eternal state at the Second Coming? A similar question could be asked about the existence of the church. Why does God cause us to be born again having all the eternal benefits that we will enjoy in the eternal state, yet leave us in an unperfected world for a period of time? Couldn't we just skip this period of life on earth? The simple answer to such questions is that it is God's will, or it serves his sovereign purpose. There are of course many other related answers to such questions as why God leaves us in an unperfected world, such as He wants us to take the gospel to the lost, or He desires to reveal his life in us to the lost world or He is using this life to disciple us so that we become more like Jesus before He takes us to himself, etc. We might even ask, why did God not just wrap up the old creation after Adam and Eve fell into sin? Why did He decide to redeem and restore it through a plan that is taking thousands of years to complete? Again, the answer to such questions is that He has so willed it, it has pleased Him to do it in this way. It must serve His greater purpose and glory. Moses tells us that God is sometimes pleased to share his reasons for what He does with us, but at other times He chooses not to reveal those reasons, "The secret things belong to the LORD our God, but the things revealed belong to us and to our sons forever" (Deut 29:29). We can take comfort in the fact that all of his reasons are determined by his infinite wisdom. The bottom line for us regarding a temple and a millennium is, what does his word reveal to us about this subject? It reveals that there will be a millennial temple, a subject I will be dealing with more detail later (cf. Isa 2:2-3; Ezek 40–48; Mic 4:1-2; Hag 2:6-7; Zech 6:12-13).

A RETURN TO THE LAW?

Another objection to the view that the Bible teaches there will be a millennium with a temple and animal sacrifices is that this necessarily implies that some sort of temple law would be in effect. If there were animal sacrifices at a temple, then it follows that the law governing those sacrifice would also be functioning. For many this is implausible for Christ fulfilled the law in his life and death. Not only has the temple disappeared, but after the death of Christ the Old Covenant with its laws has become "obsolete" (Heb 8:13). If God's work in the life of his people today under the New Covenant has advanced from the Law to life in the Spirit, then returning to the Law would be retroactive and contradictory. Doesn't Paul argue that Christ was "the end of the law" (Rom 10:4)?

This argument is based primarily on the notion that the implementation and practice of any laws similar to those found under the Old Covenant, necessarily means a return to the Mosaic Law.

For sake of space, I will just propose that in a millennial economy, laws and practices similar to those of the Mosaic system could be practiced, without the Mosaic Law again being inaugurated. Rather, these would be new laws, in some cases similar, but not under the rubric of the Mosaic Covenant. Rather they would be laws carried out in the power of the Spirit under the New Covenant. Ezekiel refers to them as "the law of the house" and "statutes of the house of the Lord," that is regulations and laws that belong to the function of the millennial temple (Ezek 43:10-12; 44:5).

Even in our age, some of the Mosaic legislation or teaching is repeated in New Testament revelation, yet that does not mean we are under the Mosaic Law. One of many examples is Paul's command in his instructions for the Ephesian church asking children to obey their parents. He then quotes from the Old Testament law, "Honor your father and mother so that it may be well with you, and that you may live long on the earth" (Exod 20:12; Eph 6:1). Thus, the Mosaic Law to honor your parents is repeated in God's revelation given to the church. But this in no way means the church is under the Mosaic Law. In a similar way, in the millennium some laws similar to the laws that Moses gave will be instituted for the new situation. But these new laws will be specific to that age, having their own purpose.

THE NEW COVENANT (NOT THE OLD) IN THE MILLENNIUM

The New Covenant was originally promised to "the house of Israel and the house of Judah" (Jer 31:31).[6] Israel as an ethnic entity ("the house of Judah and the house of Israel") has not yet entered into that covenant by faith. But this does not mean they never will. In fact, the point of Jeremiah's prophecy is that they will enter into the New Covenant at some point in the future. When they do, God's law will be written on their hearts. In Jeremiah there was no indication as to what the New Covenant law will be, rather God simply asserts, "I will put My law within them and on their heart" (Jer 31:33).

> "Behold, days are coming," declares the LORD, "when I will make a new covenant with the house of Israel and with the house of Judah, not like the covenant which I made with their fathers in the day I took them by the hand to bring them out of the land of Egypt, My covenant which they broke, although I was a husband to them," declares the LORD. "But this is the covenant which I will make with the house of Israel after those days," declares

---

6   The church, the body of Christ, made up today of both Jews and Gentiles did not begin until Pentecost (cf. Jer 31:31-34; Matt 16:18; Acts 2–4). At the Last Supper the New Covenant was announced by the Messiah and thereafter ratified through his death (Luke 22:20). Believers after Pentecost become participants in the New Covenant through faith in the Messiah (1 Cor 11:25; 2 Cor 3–4; 3:6; Heb 8:6). Ethnic Israel is yet to enter the New Covenant by embracing her Messiah.

the LORD, "I will put My law within them and on their heart I will write it; and I will be their God, and they shall be My people. "They will not teach again, each man his neighbor and each man his brother, saying, 'Know the LORD,' for they will all know Me, from the least of them to the greatest of them," declares the LORD, "for I will forgive their iniquity, and their sin I will remember no more" (Jer 31:31-34).

This covenant is in contrast to the Old Covenant, which was experienced primarily in an external way, yet it does have "law." I am proposing that the millennial temple will have laws as Ezekiel 40–48 makes clear. They are called laws, statutes, and ordinances, but they are not technically referred to as the Law of Moses and thus should not be equated with it (Ezek 36:27; 37:24; 43:11-12; 44:5, 24).

CHAPTER 7

PURPOSES

OF THE

MILLENNIUM

Paul says in Romans 11:15, "For if their [Israel's] rejection means the reconciliation of the world, what will their acceptance mean but life from the dead?" Here Paul is referring to God rejecting the Jewish nation that existed at the time of Christ because they were attempting to establish their own righteousness, and not accepting that only the righteousness of Christ would set them in a right relationship with God. If God's rejection of them led to him opening the door of the gospel to multitudes of Gentiles, then what might God's acceptance of them lead to? If God could turn such a negative event for Israel (their rejection of the Messiah) into a blessing for the world, what might He do for the world when Israel actually comes to faith? The answer Paul gave was "life from the dead," meaning eternal life for those Jews who turned in faith to their Messiah. The conversion of Israel will be the turning point for a new world order which is often referred to as the millennium.

In the history of the church, the notion of a millennium, a distinct period of time when the Messiah would rule on earth (the old earth in contrast to the new heaven and earth), has been largely rejected, based in part on the belief that the church has replaced Israel (as I discussed above). In fact, many Bible students and theologians have rejected the notion of a millennium all together. This belief is termed amillennialism, that is, no millennium. However, many amillennialists maintain there was, is, or will be a millennium of some kind. Some have believed that the millennium took place during the reigns of David and Solomon, a golden era of Old Testament Israel. Others maintained there is a millennium, but it occurs during the church age. Others have argued that the millennium will be the Messiah's rule, after his return, in the new heaven and earth, not over this old earth. There are several reasons why I believe we should seriously consider a literal thousand-year reign of Christ on this earth following his Second Coming but before the new heaven and earth.

1. To fulfill the Scriptures

The term millennium is not used in the Scripture but the phrase, "a thousand years," is applied to Christ's rule on the earth after his Second Advent. The phrase is employed six times in the space of just seven verses (Rev 20:1-7). The Old Testament prophecies that describe a coming Messiah and his rule on this earth harmonize with what Revelation 20:1-7 so succinctly states. The repetition of a *thousand years* six times in the space of just seven verses makes it hard to miss. By inspiration of the Holy Spirit, the Apostle John did not say something more or something less. He penned one *thousand years*, and he did so six times. I am not trying to be legalistic nor contentious, nor do I think it makes much difference if Christ had decided to reign on the earth for a different length of time, but if we are going to talk about how long the Messiah will rule on earth why not accept the period of time the Scripture gives us? What about that is objectionable? Revelation 20:1-7 reads as follows (notice the repetition of *a thousand years*).

Then I saw an angel coming down from heaven, holding the key of the abyss and a great chain in his hand. And he laid hold of the dragon, the serpent of old, who is the devil and Satan, and bound him for *a thousand years*; and he threw him into the abyss, and shut it and sealed it over him, so that he would not deceive the nations any longer, until *the thousand years* were completed; after these things he must be released for a short time. Then I saw thrones, and they sat on them, and judgment was given to them. And I saw the souls of those who had been beheaded because of their testimony of Jesus and because of the word of God, and those who had not worshiped the beast or his image, and had not received the mark on their forehead and on their hand; and they came to life and reigned with Christ for *a thousand years*. The rest of the dead did not come to life until *the thousand years* were completed. This is the first resurrection. Blessed and holy is the one who has a part in the first resurrection; over these the second death has no power, but they will be priests of God and of Christ and will reign with Him for *a thousand years*. When *the thousand years* are completed, Satan will be released from his prison (emphases mine).

The book of Revelation contains epistolary, prophetic and apocalyptic genres. The majority of the book consists of apocalyptic genre which is replete with symbols. It is also observable that Revelation 20 contains symbols. For example, the dragon is a symbol of Satan, and the chain symbolizes captivity, etc., but there is nothing symbolic about who Satan is; he is real. There is nothing symbolic about the abyss; it is a place of containment, nor is there anything symbolic about resurrection of the saints. Nor does there seem to be anything symbolic about the time span of a thousand years. Certain events start the period and other events end it.

73

The plain reading of this passage should lead the interpreter to understand that John wanted to emphasize a certain period of time, *a thousand years*. There is no good reason to take this to mean something other than what it clearly says. I believe that most theologians who reject the notion of a millennium do so not because they are categorically against the idea of the Messiah ruling on this earth. In fact, many hold He will literally rule on earth, that is the new heaven and earth, and I would agree with that. But rather they object to some of the specifics of what a millennium on this earth appears to entail, which I addressed previously.

Some argue that Revelation 20 is the only place in the Bible that refers specifically to a millennial rule of "a thousand years." This is true, but if Revelation 20:1-7 is inspired Scripture (I know of no believer who denies this), then this passage alone should suffice. However, there are numerous Scriptures that describe the future earthly kingdom (we call the millennial state) without using the phrase *millennium* or *a thousand years*, especially in the Old Testament prophets and in some of the Psalms. A straightforward reading of those Scriptures as we come to some of them will help clarify this. To turn these passages into descriptions of the church age or even the eternal state often does not do justice to what the author's language expresses. This, of course, takes into account any and all figures of speech as well as poetic and apocalyptic genre. We will look closely at several of these passages in the pages that follow. To conclude this point, I would argue that many Scriptures depict a millennial scene, one that does not describe our current era or the new heaven and earth.

2. To fulfill the major biblical covenants

The promises of God in the Abrahamic, Davidic, and New Covenants have not yet in their entirety been fulfilled. For example, Israel has never had uninterrupted possession of the entire land mass promised to them in the Abrahamic covenant and in later repeated promises of it (Gen 12:7; 13:14-15; 15:18-21; 17:8; 26:2-3; 28:13; 35:12; Num 34:1-15; 1 Chron 16:16-18; 2 Chron 20:6-7). Nor has the nation experienced the promised blessing which is salvation through her Messiah as intimated in the Abrahamic Covenant and spelled out in the New Covenant (Gen 12:2-3; Jer 31:31-37). Nor has Jesus, the promised Messianic king, ruled on His throne over the house of David in Jerusalem as promised (2 Sam 7:14-16; 1 Chron 17:7-14; Luke 1:31-33; Rev 5:5; 11:15). Yet these things were clearly pledged, even sworn, by God,

> My covenant I will not violate, nor will I alter the utterance of My lips. Once I have sworn by My holiness; I will not lie to David. His descendants shall endure forever and his throne as the sun before Me. It shall be established forever like the moon, and the witness in the sky is faithful." (Ps 89:34-37).

Christ's current session on his Father's throne in heaven (Heb 1:3) should not be confused with the promise that the Messiah will sit on the "throne of David" which has always been located in Jerusalem (2 Sam 3:10; 1 Kgs 2:12, 24, 45; Jer 17:25; 22:30; 29:16; 36:30). The promise given to Mary in Luke's Gospel was that Jesus would sit on and rule from the throne of David over the house of Jacob. That did not happen during his earthly ministry, nor is happening now. Instead, the Roman government, encouraged by the Jewish leaders, crucified the Messiah. But God raised Him from the dead. He ascended to the right hand of His Father. One day He will return in power and glory to reign over the house of David and the whole earth.

In the meantime, the kingdom has taken on the mystery form discussed in the parables of Matthew 13, a kingdom expressed primarily in and through the church. So, Israel has not yet experienced the fulfillment of either the Abrahamic or Davidic covenants, nor has she entered into the New Covenant which her Messiah established through his death on the cross (Luke 22:20; Heb 8:8; 12:24). The church has become a beneficiary of the New Covenant through faith in the Messiah (Luke 22:20; 1 Cor 11:25; 2 Cor 3:6; Heb 8:6-13), but it was originally promised to "the house Israel and the house of Judah" that is to Israel (Jer 31:31-34). Thus, a millennial rule allows for and creates the context for the fulfillment of God's covenant promises to Israel.

3. To fulfill the promise of an earthly (yet spiritual) kingdom on this earth with his saints

The Second Coming of Christ to earth by itself does not necessarily fulfill these covenant promises, but his in-person rule on the earth will. The kingdom originally promised to Israel in the prophets and offered to the nation by the Messiah will again be offered prior to the Second Coming,

> This gospel of the kingdom shall be preached in the whole world as a testimony to all the nations, and then the end will come (Matt 24:14).

This is not the gospel of the death and resurrection, though it will probably include it. Rather this is the good news that the kingdom is coming. This time it will be accepted and inaugurated as the Apostle John prophesies,

> The kingdom of the world has become *the kingdom* of our Lord and of His Christ; and He will reign forever and ever (Rev 11:15).

It is *this* world that Christ is destined to rule. Some argue that since this rule will be "forever and ever," it must refer to the eternal reign of Christ in the new heaven and earth. His reign on earth will certainly merge into his eternal reign, but it first begins with the millennial reign and after that moves into the eternal order. This juncture, when the millennial rule transitions into the eternal rule, is referred to by Paul where he writes,

> Then comes the end, when he delivers the kingdom to God the Father after destroying every rule and every authority and power. For he must reign until he has put all his enemies under his feet. The last enemy to be destroyed is death (1 Cor 15:24-26).

Rule in the new heaven and earth begins after Christ has destroyed all his enemies, the last rebellion is seen at the end of the millennium (Rev 20:7-10), and then death will be destroyed at the commencement of the eternal state,

> Then I saw a new heaven and a new earth; for the first heaven and the first earth passed away...there will no longer be *any* death (Rev 21:1, 4)

Before we enter that eternal state, God has promised that there is a kingdom coming to this earth,

> And the government will rest on His shoulders...There will be no end to the increase of *His* government or of peace, on the throne of David and over his kingdom, to establish it and to uphold it with justice and righteousness from then on and forevermore. The zeal of the LORD of hosts will accomplish this (Isa 9:6-7).

Again, in this passage we see the Messiah's reign on earth merge into his eternal reign. An inspection of the passages in the Old Testament that mention the "throne of David" make it readily clear that this throne was never said to be in heaven, but on earth in Jerusalem (2 Sam 3:10; 1 Kgs 2:12, 24, 45; Jer 17:25; 22:30; 29:16; 36:30).

Related to this point is God's promise that those that have followed him and suffered for him will also rule with him, "If we endure, we will also reign with Him" (2 Tim 2:12).

> You have made them *to be* a kingdom and priests to our God; and they will reign upon the earth (Rev 5:10)

The gospel is not an end in itself, but a means to an end. Without the death and resurrection of the Messiah there would be no church, no redeemed saints of the past ages, and thus none to co-rule with the Messiah in the coming kingdom. In that sense, the gospel is a means to an end: the rule of Messiah in glory upon this earth together with his saints (Zech 14:5; 1 Thess 4:14; Rev 5:10; 11:15) followed by his rule in the new heaven and earth (Rev 21–22).

4. A revelation of God's faithfulness

One very significant reason for believing in a literal fulfillment the Abrahamic, Davidic, and New Covenants, and the rule of Christ on earth for a thousand years is the faithfulness of God. It is certain that God in his word says what he means and means what he says. What he has revealed is not ambiguous. He has made literal promises. If we wait long enough, we will see that he will literally fulfill them. He must remain faithful to words and to himself. For sake of clarity, let me repeat what God states,

> My covenant I will not violate, nor will I alter the utterance of My lips. Once I have sworn by My holiness; I will not lie to David (Ps 89:34-35).

The prophet Jeremiah confirms this,

> If you can break My covenant for the day and My covenant for the night, so that day and night will not be at their appointed time, then My covenant may also be broken with David My servant so that he will not have a son to reign on his throne (Jer 33:20-21).

God's reputation as being honest and faithful, as well as clear and unambiguous, is at stake. This is not to say there is no symbolic or figurative language employed by the writers of Scripture. But it is to say that the Scriptures, a revelation of God, were written to be clear and understood. A careful reading of these texts leads to an understanding that Christ is returning to rule on the earth, *the old earth*, before He rules in the new heaven and earth in the eternal state. When John writes, "The kingdom of the world has become the kingdom of our Lord and of His Christ," it is the kingdom of *this world* not the eternal state that becomes the Lord's at that juncture in history (emphasis added). Scores, if not hundreds, of promises that God has made are described as being fulfilled upon this earth before the arrival of the eternal state. God's faithfulness and his attention to detail depends upon it.

5. To fulfill the original creation mandate

On the sixth day of the creation week, after God had created Adam and Eve, Moses wrote, "God blessed them; and God said to them, "Be fruitful and multiply, and fill the earth, and subdue it; and rule over the fish of the sea and over the birds of the sky and over every living thing that moves on the earth" (Gen 1:28). Several thousands of years after the creation, the Psalmist confirms this earlier statement:

> When I consider Your heavens, the work of Your fingers,
> The moon and the stars, which You have ordained;
> What is man that You take thought of him,
> And the son of man that You care for him?
> Yet You have made him a little lower than God,
> And You crown him with glory and majesty!
> You make him to rule over the works of Your hands;
> You have put all things under his feet,
> All sheep and oxen,

And also the beasts of the field,
The birds of the heavens and the fish of the sea,
Whatever passes through the paths of the seas (Ps 8:3-8).

Yet, the writer of Hebrews, quoting this passage, points out, "But now, we do not see all things subjection to him" (Heb 2:8). In other words, man has not fulfilled this original mandate *yet*. He has fallen short of this goal, but the writer then says, "But we do see Him who was made for a little while lower than the angels, *namely*, Jesus" (Heb 8:9). He goes on to explain that Jesus, through his death and resurrection, is bringing many "sons to glory." Paul refers to this when he says, "For the anxious longing of the creation waits eagerly for the revealing of the sons of God" (Rom 8:19).

These will be those who co-rule with him over a future subdued creation. One day all things on this earth will be subject to the rulership of man as originally planned, but it will be redeemed mankind ruling together with Christ on the earth. This kingdom will include both Jews and Gentiles, some who enter it in their natural bodies (cf. Matt 13:37-43; 25:14-21; 31-34) and others who participate in it in their resurrected glorified bodies (Matt 19:28; 1 Cor 15:35-53; Rev 2:26-27; 3:21; 20:4). Of course, the Messiah will be in his resurrected glory.

The interaction of the two categories of humans, natural and glorified, will be somewhat like Christ's post-resurrection appearances where he interacted with men and women in their earthly bodies. During the millennial state, man together with the Messiah will be able to fully subdue the earth and exercise dominion over the animal kingdom so that it will dwell in complete harmony with the human race and the creation mandate for this earth will progress to its fulfillment (cf. Gen 1:28; Isa 11:7-9; 65:11; Rev 3:21; 20:4).

6. To foil Satan's rebellion

Psalm 24:1 declares, "The earth is the Lord's, and all it contains, the world, and those who dwell in it." Psalm 89:11 confirms, "The heavens are Thine, the earth also is Thine, the world and all it contains, Thou hast founded them." Proverbs 3:19 states, "The Lord by wisdom founded the earth; by understanding He established the heavens" (Prov 3:19). However, Satan in his rebellion (Ezek 28:11-19), and subsequent leading of the human race into sin (Gen 3:1-6), became "the god of this world" and to this day it lies in his power (2 Cor 4:4; 1 John 5:19). It is in the millennial reign that God will vindicate himself, his original purpose, and his servants. Satan will be cast into the bottomless pit for the entire period (Rev 20:1-3, 7). Thus, God will no longer allow Satan to undermine his purpose and goal for human history on the earth. Rather, He will terminate Satan's rule which the Devil carried out in part through wicked earthly monarchs, and he (God) will take back the earth and the Messiah will lead mankind in fulfilling the original creation purpose.

7. To restore the earth to a state of blessing

In Colossians 1:16 Paul reveals that God was the creator of all things in heaven and earth. This includes all living things, spiritual and physical, and all inanimate creation. Sin's entrance into the creation did not just affect the human species. It apparently originated in the angelic realm (Isa 14:12-14; Ezek 28:13-18) and entered the world through Adam and Eve's disobedience (Gen 3). Sin infected the "whole creation," which includes the animal kingdom, nature, the physical earth, and the cosmos. Paul says that now, "the whole creation" groans in its fallen condition (Rom 8:22). In some way, even "heavenly things" needed to be "cleansed"—possibly referring to the need for cleansing due to Satan's defiling presence in heaven (Job 1–2; Luke 10:18; Rev 12:9).

81

Therefore it was necessary for the copies of the things in the heavens to be cleansed with these, but the heavenly things themselves with better sacrifices than these. For Christ did not enter a holy place made with hands, a *mere* copy of the true one, but into heaven itself, now to appear in the presence of God for us (Heb 9:23-24).

However far reaching the effects of sin might be, the Apostle Paul makes clear that God's plan is to reconcile "all things" to himself through Christ. This includes all things affected by the curse. This does not mean all humans will be saved nor does it mean that any rebellious angels will repent. But it does mean that the entire creation will be brought back into order, some of it by means of salvation, other parts of it by means of judgment.

For it was the *Father's* good pleasure for all the fullness to dwell in Him, and through Him to reconcile all things to Himself, having made peace through the blood of His cross; through Him, *I say*, whether things on earth or things in heaven" (Col 1:19-20).

In salvation, procured by Christ's work on the cross, the enmity between the believer and God was removed and the believer is put into a proper relationship with God. In judgment, all rebellion both demonic and human, is subdued, and every rebel will be brought into proper submission and punishment—by force.

In addition, the reconciliation of "all things" includes the act of bringing back nature to its state of blessing lost at the fall when "the creation was subject to futility" (cf. Gen 1:31; 3:1-19; Rom 8:20). The creation itself will be "set free from its slavery to corruption." (Rom 8:21). It is the old creation of Genesis 1–2 (not the new one of Rev 21–22) that needs to be set free from this corruption.

8. To finally have all peoples and nations of this world worshipping God

Throughout the Scriptures a time is promised when all nations of the earth will submit to God and gladly worship him. In his godly frustration, Jesus referred to this purpose not being fulfilled in his day, "Is it not written, 'My house shall be called a house of prayer for all the nations'? But you have made it a robber's den" (Mark 21:17). This purpose has never been fulfilled in the history of the world. Of course, this will happen in the new heaven and earth, but the Bible points to a time when this will take place in this fallen but greatly restored world before the eternal state (Isa 60:6-14; 66:18-23; Zech 14:4, 16-21).

The millennial reign will not yet be the final eternal restoration revealed in Revelation 21–22, but it will nevertheless be a greatly restored earth and humanity for some of the purposes listed above, all of which will bring glory to God. Some of the phenomenal characteristics of this restoration will be discussed later.

CHAPTER 8

PREPARATION FOR THE KINGDOM

ISRAEL'S PARTIAL RETURN TO THE LAND

For more than 1800 years the promise of a future restoration of the nation of Israel was thought to be null and void because Israel did not exist as a nation after the Roman invasion of AD 66–70. At that time the nation was destroyed, and the surviving Jews were driven from their homeland into the diaspora. For nearly two millennia, the Jewish people wandered from nation to nation and faced innumerable hardships and persecutions. In the late eighteen hundreds and the early nineteen hundreds small groups of Jews began to return to Palestine from countries all over the world. Then in 1917 during World War I, the British government issued the Balfour Declaration announcing the desire for a homeland for the Jewish people to be established in Palestine.

But it was not until after the horrific persecution of the Jews during World War II that representatives of the Jewish community in Palestine terminated the British mandate and declared Israel's independence as a new state in May of 1948. As a result of this, more Bible scholars began to reconsider the validity of the ancient promises that God had made to his people Israel. The reason for this change of mind and change of interpretation was this: After AD 70 most of the world believed the nation of Israel had experienced its final dissolution. That led many scholars, for several centuries, to believe that the Old Testament prophecies about Israel's future kingdom should be re-interpreted to apply to the church. As we discussed above, many argued that the church had replaced Israel forever as God's people. Therefore, they did not expect a literal fulfillment of the Old Testament prophecies. The prophecies were interpreted allegorically to apply to the church. Granted, the church is part of God's people, but this does not mean that God's original promises to Israel had failed or will not be fulfilled in a literal manor (Rom 9:6; Heb 4:6). Like most prophecies, if we wait long enough for God to bring them to past, we will see that He will do so, maybe not in our lifetime, but eventually in his time. Once Israel was again in their land, after 1800 years of wandering, it became plausible in the minds of a growing number of interpreters of the Bible that the Old Testament prophecies about the Jews could be fulfilled literally, and that Israel (the Jews) had not morphed into the church but remained a distinct people.

ETHNIC ISRAEL'S FUTURE CONVERSION TO THE MESSIAH

In Isaiah God expresses his supernatural patience that He had for Israel for a long time, from the time of the nation's birth until its old age (Isa 46:3-4). But when her time for salvation finally comes, the spiritual new birth will take place very rapidly,

Who has heard such a thing? Who has seen such things?

Can a land be born in one day? Can a nation be brought forth all at once? As soon as Zion travailed, she also brought forth her sons (Isa 66:8).

Zechariah is even more specific, "I will remove the iniquity of that land in one day" (Zech 3:9).

Though this perhaps indicates that the Messiah's death for Israel's sin occurred in one day, on Good Friday, the following verse refers to that day with words that depict a millennial setting, " 'In that day,' declares the LORD of hosts, 'every one of you will invite his neighbor to *sit* under *his* vine and under *his* fig tree' " (cf. Mic 4:4; Zech 3:10).

"That day" will be a time when God determines to reveal himself to the nation,

"I permitted Myself to be sought by those who did not ask *for Me*; I permitted Myself to be found by those who did not seek Me. I said, 'Here am I, here am I,' to a nation which did not call on My name" (Isa 65:1).

God will pour out his Spirit on them (cf. Ezek 36:27; 39:29; Joel 2:28-29),

"I will not hide My face from them any longer, for I will have poured out My Spirit on the house of Israel," declares the Lord GOD (Ezek 37:14).

Then they will call on the Lord for salvation,

"For then I will give to the peoples purified lips, that all of them may call on the name of the LORD" (Zeph 3:9).

This one will say, "I am the LORD's"; and that one will call on the name of Jacob; and another will write *on* his hand, "Belonging to the LORD," and will name Israel's name with honor (Isa 44:5).

The reason God saves them is not due to their goodness but rather because He had chosen the nation for salvation from the beginning (Isa 44:1-2).

> "But now listen, O Jacob, My servant, and Israel, whom I have chosen: thus says the LORD who made you and formed you from the womb, who will help you, Do not fear, O Jacob My servant; and you Jeshurun whom I have chosen" (Isa 44:1-2).

Numerous prophetic statements in the Old Testament Scriptures indicate that Israel will enter into the New Covenant at the time of her repentance and conversion to her Messiah. Jeremiah 31 is probably the most notable passage that predicts the New Covenant.

> "Behold, days are coming," declares the LORD, "when I will make a new covenant with the house of Israel and with the house of Judah, not like the covenant which I made with their fathers in the day I took them by the hand to bring them out of the land of Egypt, My covenant which they broke, although I was a husband to them," declares the LORD. "But this is the covenant which I will make with the house of Israel after those days," declares the LORD, "I will put My law within them and on their heart I will write it; and I will be their God, and they shall be My people (Jer 31:31-33).

This covenant is understood in contrast to the Old Covenant which God made through Moses with Israel at Mount Sinai (Exod 19:3-8; 24:3-8). In that covenant the people of Israel entered into a bilateral agreement where God laid down the stipulations, blessings, and curses and the people of Israel agreed to keep all the covenant. Whereas the Abrahamic Covenant recorded the eternal promises God made to the descendants of

Abraham, the Mosaic Covenant regulated the nation's life with God through temporary blessings and curses dependent upon the people's obedience.

Throughout their history, Israel continually violated the Mosaic Covenant and reaped the judgment curses of that agreement. The only reason the nation did not totally perish in judgment was God's faithfulness to his Abrahamic promises. To this day, after thousands of years of history, the Abrahamic Covenant remains intact and because of those promises, God has preserved his nation. The New Covenant issues out of the original Abrahamic promises. Israel will yet one day enter into the New Covenant promised in Jeremiah 31 and Ezekiel 36–37.

In Ezekiel 36, the prophet characterizes a time that could not refer to the post-exilic period after the Babylonian captivity under Zerubbabel, Ezra, and Nehemiah, for he says in verse 15, "'I will not let you hear insults from the nations anymore, nor will you bear disgrace from the peoples any longer, nor will you cause your nation to stumble any longer,' declares the Lord GOD." Under Zerubbabel, Ezra, and Nehemiah the nation did continue to face immense opposition from the surrounding peoples and did stumble into sin. So Ezekiel is not referring to that post-exilic period but rather to a yet future day:

> For I will take you from the nations, gather you from all the lands and bring you into your own land. Then I will sprinkle clean water on you, and you will be clean; I will cleanse you from all your filthiness and from all your idols. Moreover, I will give you a new heart and put a new spirit within you; and I will remove the heart of stone from your flesh and give you a heart of flesh. I will put My Spirit within you and cause you to walk in My statutes, and you will be careful to observe My ordinances. You will live in the land that I gave to your forefathers;

so you will be My people, and I will be your God (Ezek 36:24-28).

God's promise to give them a new heart and cause them to walk in his law, harmonizes with what Jeremiah said in his promise of the new covenant (Jer 31:31-33). Ezekiel refers to this covenant as the "covenant of peace" (Ezek 37:26). Both prophets mention that at that point Israel will be God's people, and He will be their God (Jer 31:33-34; Ezek 37:28). The cleansing that Ezekiel mentions refers to the repentance and conversion of the nation to YHWH though the pouring out of his Spirit (Ezek 36:25).

From among the prophets, Zechariah gives the greatest detail about the nation's conversion. He says a day will come when the Spirit of God will be poured out, specifically on the house of David and Levi, and one family after another will weep in repentance embracing their Messiah (Zech 12:10-13:1).

I will pour out on the house of David and on the inhabitants of Jerusalem, the Spirit of grace and of supplication, so that they will look on Me whom they have pierced; and they will mourn for Him, as one mourns for an only son, and they will weep bitterly over Him like the bitter weeping over a firstborn. In that day there will be great mourning in Jerusalem, like the mourning of Hadadrimmon in the plain of Megiddo. The land will mourn, every family by itself; the family of the house of David by itself and their wives by themselves; the family of the house of Nathan by itself and their wives by themselves; the family of the house of Levi by itself and their wives by themselves; the family of the Shimeites by itself and their wives by themselves; all the families that remain, every family by itself and their wives by themselves. In that day a fountain will be opened for the house of David and for the inhabitants of Jerusalem, for sin and for impurity.

The key thing to see here is that this repentance is toward the Messiah, the one they "pierced," whom the Lord identifies as "Me" (Zech 12:10). This is the point where "The stone which the builders rejected has become the chief corner stone" (Ps 118:22). Israel will realize that Jesus whom they rejected was truly their Messiah.

This event appears to accompany a horrific event in Israel's future, an invasion of Jerusalem by foreign armies (Zech 12:2; 14:2). Paul confirms that "all Israel will be saved" that is those that have turned in repentance to the Messiah (Rom 11:26-27). This conversion follows a long period of hardness of heart by Israel towards her Messiah (Isa 45:25; 60:21; Rom 11:25). It will be the time when Israel will finally say, "Blessed is he who comes in the name of the Lord" (Matt 23:39). The prophet Zechariah reveals that at that time one third of the Jewish population in the land of Israel will be saved and the other two thirds destroyed,

> In the whole land, declares the LORD, two thirds shall be cut off and perish, and one third shall be left alive. And I will put this third into the fire, and refine them as one refines silver, and test them as gold is tested. They will call upon my name, and I will answer them. I will say, 'They are my people'; and they will say, 'The LORD is my God' (Zech 13:8-9).

When Paul says in Romans 11:26 that "all Israel will be saved," he is referring to those who survive and turn in faith to the Messiah. He goes on to describe the situation, "The Deliverer will come from Zion, he will banish ungodliness from Jacob."

This event of Israel's conversion to Messiah, takes place on the heels of an invasion of the nation. God intervenes to destroy the invading army and to save Israel. Ezekiel says that the invasion will take place "in the last days" (Ezek 38:16). God will make himself "known among many nations" (Ezek 38:23).

"From that day onward," Israel will know God and the Messiah (Ezek 39:7, 22, 28). In the midst of this conversion, Matthew says that Christ will return "with power and great glory" (Matt 24:30). Zechariah tells us that his feet will touch down on the Mount of Olives,

> In that day His feet will stand on the Mount of Olives, which is in front of Jerusalem on the east (Zech 14:4).

The main point I want us to see is that from the fall of man in Genesis 3, God had promised to restore the earth to blessing. He promised a Messiah and a kingdom. The kingdom that was promised to David, announced by the prophets, offered by the Messiah, and originally rejected by Israel is still on track and will come to fruition when Israel finally repents and embraces her Messiah.

The prophet Micah characterizes this as a time when Israel will be forgiven all her sins, "He will again have compassion on us; he will tread our iniquities under foot. Yes, You will cast all their sins into the depths of the sea" (Mic 7:19).

At his return, the binding and casting of Satan into the abyss for "a thousand years" will set the stage for the establishment of the millennial kingdom on the earth (Rev 19:11–20:7):

> And he laid hold of the dragon, the serpent of old, who is the devil and Satan, and bound him for a thousand years; and he threw him into the abyss, and shut it and sealed it over him, so that he would not deceive the nations any longer, until the thousand years were completed; after these things he must be released for a short time (Rev 20:2-3).

CHAPTER 9

ESTABLISHING THE KINGDOM OF GOD ON EARTH

The means by which the direct rule of Christ is brought to earth is violent. The rulers of the earth are not willing to simply lay aside their power and submit themselves to the omnipotent King. In fact, they will fight him with all of their strength, "The kings of the earth and their armies assembled to make war against Him who sat on the horse and against His army" (Rev 19:19). Their kingdoms must be wrenched from them by force. The prophet Daniel says that God's kingdom "will crush and put an end to all these kingdoms, but it will itself endure forever" (Dan 2:44). God initiates this process of tearing the kingdoms of the world out of the hands of worldly kings in the Day of the Lord, a period of catastrophic judgment which is portrayed by many of the prophets and unfolds in great detail in the last book of the Bible (Rev 6–19). In one judgment alone one third of the earth's population is decimated (Rev 9:15, 18). The psalmist summarizes the build-up to the Second Coming,

The nations made an uproar, the kingdoms tottered; He raised His voice, the earth melted...Come, behold the works of the LORD, who has wrought desolations in the earth (Ps 46:6, 8).

Jesus said it will be, "a great tribulation, such as has not occurred since the beginning of the world until now, nor ever will. Unless those days had been cut short, no life would have been saved" (Matt 24:21-22).[7]

Zechariah declares concerning the armies that come against Jerusalem at that time, "And in that day I will set about to destroy all the nations that come against Jerusalem" (Zech 12:9). John adds, regarding the armies left standing at the descent of the Lord from heaven, "The rest were killed with the sword which came from the mouth of him who sat on the horse" (Rev 19:21). Jeremiah emphasizes that the extent of these judgments will be the whole earth,

"A clamor has come to the end of the earth, because the LORD has a controversy with the nations. He is entering into judgment with all flesh; as for the wicked, He has given them to the sword," declares the LORD. Thus says the LORD of hosts, "Behold, evil is going forth from nation to nation, and a great storm is being stirred up from the remotest parts of the earth. Those slain by the LORD on that day will be from one end of the earth to the other. They will not be lamented, gathered or buried; they will be like dung on the face of the ground" (Jer 25:31-33).

---

7   According to the book of Revelation, these events take place in a seven-year period of judgment that parallels the seventieth week (seven years) spoken of by the prophet Daniel. This seven-year period is divided into two parts of three and one-half years each (Dan 9:27; Rev 11:2-3; 12:6, 14; 13:5). Three different descriptions for the three and one-half years are: (1)1260 days (Rev 11:3; 12:6), (2) 42 months (Rev 11:2: 13:5), or (3) time, times, and half a time (Dan 7:25). Jeremiah called this "the time of Jacob's trouble" (Jer 30:7). Other biblical writers sometimes refer to it as "the Day of the Lord" and depict it as a time of wrath and judgment (cf. Isa 2:12; 13:9-13; 24:1-6, 21; Joel 2:10-11; Zeph 1:2-3,14-16; 1 Thess 5:1-11, 2 Thess 2:1-12; Rev 6:17).

At this time, some of the Jewish people still scattered worldwide will refuse to accept Jesus as their Messiah. Ezekiel says that God's judgment will separate them out from those who embrace the returning King, and they will not enter the coming kingdom,

"And I will purge from you the rebels and those who transgress against Me; I will bring them out of the land where they sojourn, but they will not enter the land of Israel" (Ezek 20:38).

Jesus expresses the same point in the parable of the wheat and the tares. He says believers and non-believers will live together until he comes to separate them at the end of the age, the Second Coming,

Allow both to grow together until the harvest; and in the time of the harvest I will say to the reapers, "First gather up the tares and bind them in bundles to burn them up; but gather the wheat into my barn" (Matt 13:30).

In verses 49-50 he gives his interpretation of the parable, "So it will be at the end of the age; the angels will come forth and take out the wicked from among the righteous, and will throw them into the furnace of fire; in that place there will be weeping and gnashing of teeth." The gathering of the "wheat into my barn" refers to the believers who survived the period of judgment and enter the kingdom.

In Matthew 24, the Olivet Discourse explains the judgment and build up to the Second Coming. In the following chapter Jesus refers not to the eternal state but to his occupying the Davidic throne,

But when the Son of Man comes in His glory, and all the angels with Him, then He will sit on His glorious throne (Matt 25:31).

In the next verses he says that he will separate "the sheep from the goats." To the sheep he says, "Come you who are blessed of My Father, inherit the kingdom prepared for you from the foundation of the world" (Matt 25:32-34). To the goats he says, "Depart from Me, accursed ones, into the eternal fire which has been prepared for the devil and his angels" (Matt 25:41).

My reason for pointing this out is to say that at the beginning of the earthly reign of Christ, there will be a greatly decimated earth and greatly reduced population due to the judgments. At the return of Christ all the remaining unbelievers will be brought to judgment as well as all resistant nations (Matt 13:49; 25:31-46). Those believers left alive from the Jews and the Gentiles, will enter into the millennial kingdom in their physical bodies. Daniel seems to indicate it will take a couple months to complete these judgments and to begin the rebuilding work (Dan 12:11-12). But the main point to see here is that only believers from both Jews and Gentiles who survived the period of judgment will be allowed to enter that kingdom. But they will do so in their earthly bodies.

> This will begin his rule on the earth as projected in Revelation 11:15:

> The kingdom of the world has become *the kingdom* of our Lord and of His Christ; and He will reign forever and ever.

Revelation 20 specifically says that Christ will rule on this earth a thousand years. After that, it is not that his reign changes, but the earth changes. It is startling how little is said about the millennial reign in chapter 20. Rather, John jumps quickly over it to the new heaven and earth in the final two chapters of the Bible. But perhaps he did so because the actual details of the millennial kingdom, which are many, are spread throughout the Old Testament in the Psalms and Prophets. Those writers of Scripture held out this hope like a burning torch. Now it has finally arrived.

My purpose in the following pages is to describe in some detail some of the salient features of the millennial reign as depicted in broad array of Scriptures. I will attempt to show this by citing excerpts that range from Genesis to Revelation, but focusing on the contribution of certain Psalms, and selected passages from Isaiah, Ezekiel, and to a lesser extent from the other prophets, and the New Testament.

CHAPTER 10

GOVERNMENTAL FEATURES OF THE KINGDOM

THE BINDING OF SATAN

Satan who caused much deception and devastation through-out history among the nations and their leaders will be bound and cast into the abyss,

> Then I saw an angel coming down from heaven, holding the key of the abyss and a great chain in his hand. And he laid hold of the dragon, the serpent of old, who is the devil and Satan, and bound him for a thousand years and he threw him into the abyss, and shut *it* and sealed *it* over him, so that he would not deceive the nations any longer, until the thousand years were completed (Rev 20:1-3).

Among his wicked works, three of the foremost are murder, lying, and deception (Gen 3:1; John 8:44; Rev 20:3).

Job 1–2, Daniel 10, and Revelation 6–16 reveal that under the sovereign hand of God Satan has at times been granted power to afflict with disease, energize armies for evil aims, and bring about catastrophes such as earthquakes and tornadoes (Job 1:15-19; 2:7). In the abyss, he will no longer be allowed to do any of these malevolent things.

The abyss appears to be the location where other wicked angels (demons), whose rebellion was severe in pre-Flood history, have been incarcerated (1 Pet 3:18; 2 Pet 2:6; Jude 6). During the ministry of Christ, Satan and his angels knew of this place and feared it greatly (Luke 8:31). No longer harassed by Satan or his demons, mankind will be able to finally thrive and fulfill God's original creation mandate. Satan will be confined for the entire period (Rev 20:1-8).

THE RETURN OF GOD'S PROTECTIVE GLORY

Moses pleaded with God, "Show me Your glory" (Exod 33:18-23). The psalmist had a similar desire, "One thing I have asked from the LORD, that I shall seek: that I may dwell in the house of the Lord all the days of my life, to behold the beauty of the Lord" (Ps 27:4). Like Moses and the psalmist, an innate desire of every believer is to see Christ in his glory. Christ also desires to reveal his glory to the church, "Father, I desire that they also, whom You have given Me, be with Me where I am, so that they may see My glory which You have given Me for You loved Me before the foundation of the world" (John 17:24). A distinctive feature of the millennial reign is that the glory of God that dwelt in ancient Israel will physically manifest itself again in Jerusalem.

We saw the glory of God first come to Israel during the Exodus in the form of a cloud by day and fire by night (Exod 13:20-22). It protected the fledgling nation from attack by the Egyptians (Exod 14:19-20). Later it entered into Solomon's temple (1 Kgs 8:3). At the collapse of the kingdom, it departed the temple and city, signifying the removal of God's immediate presence. God gave the prophet Ezekiel a vision of the glory as it departed from the temple in Jerusalem just prior to the Babylonian captivity. The glory moved from above the cherubim, which were part of the Ark of the Covenant in the Holy of Holies of the temple to the temple courtyard, and then to the mountain east of the city which is the Mount of Olives. Then the glory departed the city (Ezek 8–11). The glory did not return to the rebuilt temple at the time of Ezra and Haggai.

During the earthly ministry of Christ, his glory was both revealed and veiled. The Apostle John states, "We saw His glory, glory as of the only begotten from the Father." He could have been referring to the glory manifested at the transfiguration (cf. Matt 17:2-8; Mark 9:2-8; Luke 9:28-30), but if that was the case, it would seem strange that John alone of the Gospel writers did not record the transfiguration episode. More likely the glory that John was referring to was the fact that Jesus was "full of grace and truth" (John 1:14). This revelation of his glory would be focusing on the excellence of Jesus' divine character. All three of the Synoptic writers record the transfiguration of Jesus with Peter, James and John present. Matthew writes, "He was transfigured before them; and His face shone like the sun, and His garments became as white as light" (Matt 17:2), and they also were enveloped by the cloud of his glory (Matt 17:5; Luke 9:34-35). Luke states, "the appearance of His face became different, and His clothing *became* white *and* gleaming" and "they saw his glory" (Luke 9:29, 32). Peter refers to the experience in his second epistle (2 Pet 1:16-18). But apart from the transfiguration, the glory of God did not appear in the form of light and majestic splendor in the Gospel narratives. In that sense, it was veiled. But his glory revealed itself in other ways—through his words, character, and miraculous works. Jesus noted that he dwelt in glory before the creation of the world and that he would return to that state through his resurrection and ascension into heaven (John 17:5).

It is not until the Second Coming of Christ that the glory of God, present in Israel's past theocracy, takes up residence again on the earth, "And then the sign of the Son of Man will appear in the sky, and then all the tribes of the earth will mourn, and they will see the son of man coming on the clouds of the sky with power and great glory" (Matt 24:30). It is significant that the prophet Zechariah reveals that when the Messiah returns in glory, his feet will touch down on the Mount of Olives. The very place where the glory departed—to that location it will return (cf. Ezek 11:23; Zech 14:3-4). The return of Christ in glory will signal the establishment of his messianic rule, "But when the Son of Man comes in His glory, and all the angels with Him, then He will sit on His glorious throne" (Matt 24:31). More specifically it will signify the restoration of the Davidic kingdom in Israel (Isa 4:3-6; Ezek 43:1-4; Zech 2:5; 14:3-4; Matt 24:29-30).

In his vision, the prophet Isaiah sees the return of God's glory to Israel,

> Arise, shine; for your light has come, and the glory of the LORD has risen upon you. For behold, darkness will cover the earth and deep darkness the peoples; but the LORD will rise upon you and His glory will appear upon you. Nations will come to your light, and kings to the brightness of your rising (Isa 60:1-3).

Isaiah also refers to the glory cloud functioning as a canopy of protection over Zion, the temple area in Jerusalem, in the reconstituted nation,

> Then the LORD will create over the whole area of Mount Zion and over her assemblies a cloud by day, even smoke, and the brightness of a flaming fire by night; for over all the glory will be a canopy (Isa 2:5).

The prophet Zechariah agrees with this,

'For I,' declares the LORD, 'will be a wall of fire around her, and I will be the glory in her midst' (Zech 2:5).

It is improbable that this refers to the eternal state because the walls around the New Jerusalem will not be of fire but of precious stones (cf. Rev 21:9-21).

Ezekiel chronicles the entrance of God's glory into the millennial temple which will be built after Christ's return:

Then he led me to the gate, the gate facing toward the east; and behold, the glory of the God of Israel was coming from the way of the east. And His voice was like the sound of many waters; and the earth shone with His glory. And *it was* like the appearance of the vision which I saw, like the vision which I saw when He came to destroy the city [the Babylonian invasion]. And the visions *were* like the vision which I saw by the river Chebar; and I fell on my face. And the glory of the LORD came into the house by the way of the gate facing toward the east. And the Spirit lifted me up and brought me into the inner court; and behold, the glory of the LORD filled the house (Ezek 43:1-5).

It is noteworthy that Ezekiel is the prophet who links the returning glory with the glory that departed the city at the Babylonian captivity. It is the same glory that will return in the person and ministry of Christ (Ezek 11:23; 43:1-5).

The psalmist tells us that once God's glory has returned to Jerusalem, it will be visible to all who worship there.

So the nations will fear the name of the LORD and all the kings of the earth Your glory. For the LORD has built up Zion; He has appeared in His glory (Ps 102:15-16).

The psalmist knew he was speaking about the future era for he says just two verses later, "This will be written for the generation to come, that a people yet to be created may praise the LORD" (Ps 102:18).

CHRIST IS THE ONE KING OVER ALL THE EARTH

Never in world history has there been a single ruler who has ruled over every nation of the earth. But "the earth is the Lord's," therefore He alone has the right to do so (cf. Ps 24:1; Rev 5:12). This right is reserved for Him since He is both its creator and redeemer (Gen 1:1; Rev 4:10; 5:9-10). The writers of Scripture make very clear that the Messiah's reign will be over every nation of the earth. This is hardly the case today. Christ does rule in the hearts of believers today but not directly over the nations. Even though he is in sovereign control of them, his direct and immediate rule over them is reserved for that period after he returns (Rev 20:4). This is expressed clearly in Revelation 11:15,

> The kingdom of the world has become *the kingdom* of our Lord and of His Christ (cf. Dan 2:44-45; 7:26-27).

The prophet Zechariah notes that at this point in world history Christ will be the only Lord having no competition from either idols or false religions,

> And the LORD will be king over all the earth; in that day the LORD will be *the only* one, and His name *the only* one (Zech 14:9).

A thousand years before the First Advent, the psalmists depict this same future setting,

> All the ends of the earth will remember and turn to the LORD, and all the families of the nations will worship before You. For the kingdom is the LORD's and He rules over the nations (Ps 22:27-28).

May He also rule from sea to sea and from the River {Euphrates] to the ends of the earth, and Let...all kings bow down before Him, all nations serve Him (Ps 72:8,11).

And let all kings bow down before Him, all nations serve Him (Ps 72:11).

All nations whom You have made shall come and worship before You, O Lord, and they shall glorify Your name (Ps 86:9).

Some have tried to argue that such passages merely describe God's sovereign rule over the nations, but never in the history of the world have all the families and nations of the earth in any fashion bowed before, worshiped, and served God. More likely the psalmists were projecting the millennial rule of the Messiah.

The prophet Malachi envisions this same condition,

For from the rising of the sun even to its setting, My name *will be* great among the nations, and in every place incense is going to be offered to My name, and a grain offering *that is* pure; for My name *will be* great among the nations," says the LORD of hosts.

Zechariah confirms this same hope, "His dominion will be from sea to sea, and from the River [Euphrates] to the ends of the earth" (Zech 9:10). In speaking of this transfer of power from the kingdoms of the world to the Messiah, the prophet Daniel says, "And to Him was given dominion, glory and a kingdom, that all the peoples, nations and *men of every* language might serve Him" (Dan 7:14).

Jesus will be the supernatural monarch of the world. The seat of Messiah's government will be centered in Jerusalem, "At that time they will call Jerusalem 'The Throne of the LORD,' and all the nations will be gathered to it" (Jer 3:17). The psalmist calls it

"Zion…the city of the Great King" (Ps 48:2). Zion is that area in Jerusalem where the Davidic kings lived and ruled. From there Messiah will rule the world, He will send "forth His command to the earth; His word runs very swiftly" (Ps 2:6; 147:15).

Once Christ begins this reign, it will never be taken from him, "There will be no end to the increase of *His* government or of peace, On the throne of David and over His kingdom" (Isa 9:7). The eternality of his reign was confirmed to Mary at the announcement of Jesus' birth, "The Lord God will give to him the throne of his father David, and he will reign over the house of Jacob forever, and of his kingdom there will be no end" (Luke 1:32-33). John makes the point succinctly, "He shall reign forever and ever" (Rev 11:15).[8]

The Messiah's reign is forever but this does not mean that the millennium equates with the eternal state. Rather it means that what begins in the millennium will continue on into eternity without interruption. It is helpful and important to see that this reign begins at the Second Coming of Christ to earth and will continue on earth for a thousand years, but then will transition seamlessly into eternity, with the creation of the new heaven and earth (Rev 20:1-7; 21:1).

This implies that the kingdom will be absolutely secure for the entire millennial period:

And his throne as the sun before Me, it shall be established forever like the moon, and the witness in the sky is faithful (Ps 89:35-36).

It is perhaps worth noting that there may be no sun or moon in the new heaven and earth, "The city has no need of the sun or of the moon" (Rev 21:23). But during the millennial period the sun and moon will function as faithfully as they do today.

---

8   See my discussion on the meaning of the Hebrew term "forever" (*'olam*) on pages 140 and 141. Depending on context, its meaning can range from a long duration to eternity.

As constant and faithful as they are, so will be his reign. Since
this rule is forever, it will proceed from the millennial state right
into the eternal state. It is true that Satan will be let loose from
his imprisonment at the end of the millennial period and lead
a rebellion, but that revolt will not be successful in interrupting
the Messiah's rule. Rather, his uprising will be squelched before
it accomplishes any damage to the Messiah's realm (Rev 20:10).
In fact, it may be that the rebellion at the end comes only from
certain Gentile nations, for once Israel is saved at the beginning
of the millennium, it appears the nation shall remain faithful for
the duration of it,

> "As for Me, this is My covenant with them," says the
> LORD: My Spirit which is upon you, and My words
> which I have put in your mouth shall not depart from
> your mouth, nor from the mouth of your offspring, nor
> from the mouth of your offspring's offspring," says the
> LORD, "from now and forever" (cf. Isa 59:21; 60:21).

Thus, it can be said that the Messiah's rule on earth which
began at the beginning of the millennium will be forever, since
it will continue uninterrupted on into the new heaven and earth.

Overviewing God's kingdom from our current perspective,
the mystery form of it is manifested today in the church, this
will be followed by the Messiah's millennial rule on the earth,
and then following that will be the creation of the new heaven
and earth. The term "kingdom" is not used in Revelation 21–22
in referring to the eternal state but the term "reign" is (Rev 22:5).
Paul's comment in 1 Corinthians 15:24-28 is helpful in seeing
this transition from the end of the millennium into eternity.

> Then comes the end, when He hands over the kingdom to
> the God and Father, when He has abolished all rule and
> all authority and power. For He must reign until He has
> put all His enemies under His feet. The last enemy that

will be abolished is death. For He has put all things in subjection under his feet. But when He says, "All things are put in subjection," it is evident that He is excepted who put all things in subjection to Him. When all things are subjected to Him, then the Son Himself also will be subjected to the One who subjected all things to Him, so that God may be all in all.

Concerning his rule, Paul says above, "For He must reign until He has put all His enemies under His feet, the last enemy that will be abolished is death" (vv. 25-26). Since death will not be done away with until after the thousand years, Paul must be referring to Christ millennial reign when he says, "He must reign." Part of the purpose of the millennial reign will be to abolish "all [demonic and earthly] rule and authority and power" that is pitted against God (v. 24) and to "put all things in subjection under his feet (v. 27). It is after this messianic accomplishment that the "end" of the millennium comes and the Messiah "hands over the kingdom to the God and Father" (v. 24).

CHRIST WILL SHARE HIS RULE WITH RESURRECTED OLD AND NEW TESTAMENT SAINTS

The most significant feature of the millennial period is that Christ will reign over the whole world. But nearly as astounding is the biblical teaching that the redeemed, "from every tribe and tongue and people and nation" will rule with him. This is not referring to a heavenly rule but rather his rule "on the earth" (Rev 5:9-10).

Throughout the ages, God's saints have been treated horrifically. In general, they have not ruled but been ruled over and mostly by tyrants who persecuted, and even tortured and murdered them. But the is day coming when Christ will vindicate his people from all ages. He will raise them from the dead and grant them eternal resurrection bodies in which they will rule with Him. There are occasional hints of a future resurrection in the Old Testament. For example, in the midst of his bitter trial Job exclaimed, "As for me, I know that my Redeemer lives, and at the last He will take His stand on the earth. Even after my skin is destroyed, yet from my flesh I shall see God" (Job 19:25-26). Notice the redeemer's stand will be "on the earth" not in heaven.

One of the reasons Abraham was able to obey God's command to offer up his only son was that he believed God was able to raise Isaac from the dead, "He considered that God is able to raise *people* even from the dead" (Heb 11:19). David also believed in the resurrection, for in Acts 2:24-28 the Apostle Peter reveals that David understood that God would raise the Messiah and not allow his body to go through the normal decay of death, "For You will not abandon my soul to Sheol; nor will You allow Your Holy One to undergo decay" (cf. Ps 16:10). Peter then noted that David was prophesying about the resurrection of the Messiah (Acts 2:30-31). Isaiah and Ezekiel also prophesied of a future resurrection (cf. Isa 26:19; Ezek 37:1-14), but it is the prophet Daniel who most poignantly reveals the resurrection of the saints,

> Many of those who sleep in the dust of the ground will awake, these to everlasting life, but the others to disgrace and everlasting contempt. Those who have insight will shine brightly like the brightness of the expanse of heaven, and those who lead the many to righteousness, like the stars forever and ever (Dan 12:2-3).

Jesus reiterated that for those who responded to him in faith there will a resurrection to life and for those who rejected him a resurrection to judgment, "Do not marvel at this; for an hour is coming, in which all who are in the tombs will hear His voice, and will come forth; those who did the good deeds to a resurrection of life, those who committed the evil deeds to a resurrection of judgment" (John 5:28-29). His point was not that good deeds earn eternal life but that they were proof that one possessed eternal life through faith in the Messiah. Jesus not only taught there will be a resurrection, but he even said of himself,

> I am the resurrection and the life; he who believes in Me will live even if he dies (John 11:25).

At one point in his earthly ministry Jesus promised to his apostles that they would one day rule over the twelve tribes of Israel. "Truly I say to you, that you who have followed Me, in the regeneration when the Son of Man will sit on His glorious throne, you also shall sit upon twelve thrones, judging the twelve tribes of Israel" (Matt 19:27-30). That did not take place in their lifetime nor is it now taking place in heaven, but it will occur on the earth when he raises them from the dead to rule with him.

In addition, the Apostle Paul taught that the entire body of Christ, the church will also be raised,

> For the Lord Himself will descend from heaven with a shout, with the voice of the archangel and with the trumpet of God, and the dead in Christ will rise first. Then we who are alive and remain will be caught up together with them in the clouds to meet the Lord in the air, and so we shall always be with the Lord" (1 Thess 4:16-17).

Whether the Lord is in heaven or is ruling on the earth, we will always be with him. Paul clarifies that our resurrection is as certain as Christ's (1 Cor 15:16) and that it will be instantaneous, "In a moment, in the twinkling of an eye, at the last trumpet; for the trumpet will sound, and the dead will be raised imperishable, and we will be changed" (1 Cor 15:52).

According to Revelation 20:4, immediately after Christ returns, a resurrection of those that died for him as martyrs will take place:

Then I saw thrones, and they sat on them, and judgment was given to them. And I *saw* the souls of those who had been beheaded because of their testimony of Jesus and because of the word of God, and those who had not worshiped the beast or his image, and had not received the mark on their forehead and on their hand; and they came to life and reigned with Christ for a thousand years. The rest of the dead did not come to life until the thousand years were completed. This is the first resurrection. Blessed and holy is the one who has a part in the first resurrection; over these the second death has no power, but they will be priests of God and of Christ and will reign with Him for a thousand years (Rev 20:4-6).

This summary of the resurrection of the saints covers both Old and New Testament believers. In Revelation 5:9-10, John makes clear that the sphere in which the saints will reign is "on the earth,"

You were slain, and purchased for God with Your blood men from every tribe and tongue and people and nation. You have made them to be a kingdom and priests to our God; and *they will reign upon the earth* (emphasis added).

Without going into the specifics of the arguments for the chronological order of the resurrections, it is simply important to see that the saints will be raised and will participate in Christ's reign by co-ruling with Him. How could Christ promise the church at Thyatira that they would rule with Him if he did not plan to raise them from the dead to participate in that rule (Rev 2:27)? This presupposes then that in the millennium those in resurrected and glorified bodies will intermingle with those who populate the kingdom in their natural earthly bodies, much in the same way that Christ had fellowship with His disciples after His resurrection. He was in His raised body; they were in their

111

mortal bodies. Sharing in the blessings of the kingdom will be a privilege for both Old and New Testament saints. The writer of Hebrews reveals that it was God's purpose to have all of his saints, past and present, share together in Christ's reward, "Because God had provided something better for us, so that apart from us they would not be made perfect" (Heb 11:40).

If we endure, we will also reign with Him (2 Tim 2:12).

Justice is Served: A Government of Righteousness and Justice

From the beginning of human history, the desire of all the peoples of all the nations has been for a government that rules justly, judges that deliver fair and unbiased verdicts, police that act fairly and take no bribes. Finally, that day will come when absolute justice rules over the entire earth. In its history, Jerusalem, the capital of Israel, the land of his chosen people, had been vile and corrupt (Ezek 16; 23). More than once, God had to bring severe judgment upon the city and the nation. But a day is coming when the city will be called, "the city of righteousness, a faithful city" (Isa 1:27).

To cite Isaiah again, he says of Messiah's government, "There will be no end to the increase of *His* government or of peace, on the throne of David and over his kingdom, to establish it and to uphold it with justice and righteousness" (Isa 9:7). It will be a government in which "justice and righteousness" prevail. When any rebellion or criminality arises within the realm, the Lord will mete out justice firmly, "He will rule them with a rod of iron" (Ps 2:9; Rev 2:27; 19:15). Though conditions in the world will be greatly and wonderfully changed, children born in the millennium will still possess a fallen sinful nature, passed on from the time of Adam and will themselves need to be saved from the penalty of their sins through faith in the Messiah. Individuals and nations that overtly rebel against the Lord in the millennium will face swift judgment and justice (Ps 72:4; Zech 14:16-19).

This is hardly a picture of the eternal state in the new heaven and earth but rather depicts his rule on earth during the millennium. Messiah's judgments will not be merely external, rather he will also take into account heart motives in rendering fair decisions, "And He will delight in the fear of the LORD, and He will not judge [merely] by what His eyes see, nor make a decision [merely] by what His ears hear; but with righteousness He will judge the poor, and decide with fairness for the afflicted of the earth" (Isa 11:3-4). If there are afflicted people, this cannot be describing the new heaven and earth. It is in the Messiah's millennial reign that he will swiftly bring justice to the afflicted.

Also, he will intervene quickly to rescue those facing any need, "He will deliver the needy when he cries for help, the afflicted also, and him who has no helper" (Ps 72:12). Again, this cannot be describing the new heaven and new earth because there we will be no poor, afflicted, needy, or cries for help. "Before they call I will answer; while they are yet speaking I will hear" (Isa 65:24). Isaiah sums it up succinctly, "He will faithfully bring forth justice. He will not be disheartened or crushed until He has established justice in the earth" (Isa 42:3-4).

During the time of the Old Testament kings, God did not judge the wicked immediately or even every day, but in Psalm 101, God says a day is coming when, "He who practices deceit shall not dwell within my house; He who speaks falsehood shall not maintain his position before me. Every morning I will destroy all the wicked of the land, so as to cut off from the city of the LORD all those who do iniquity" (Ps 101:7-8). This apparently will be a literal reality when Christ rules.

Not only will the Messiah be just, but there will also be no corruption among his government officials (those that are ruling under him), "Behold, a king will reign righteously, and princes will rule justly" (Isa 32:1). Ezekiel calls the millennial princes to a strict standard of justice in their weights and measurements

(Ezek 45:9-12). This level of justice has never existed in human history but it will in the millennial period.

JOY TO THE WORLD

At Christmas time we often sing the old hymn "Joy to the World," written by Isaac Watts in 1719 and based on the angel's announcement at the birth of Christ, "Do not be afraid; for behold, I bring you good news of great joy which will be for all the people" (Luke 2:10). Indeed, there is great joy for every individual who has come to know Christ and His salvation, but for the world in general the experience of joy has been sporadic at best and short-lived. But a day is coming when the world will experience unprecedented joy, both in Jerusalem and among the nations of the earth.

Today Jerusalem is hardly a city of joy. Israel is a land that has been full of strife since its founding. Only for very brief periods of time have the inhabitants experienced peace. Of course, in recent decades Christians have rejoiced in visiting the city, but the inhabitants have never really had rest or security from outside enemies. Groups or nations have always been threatening, planning, or carrying out attacks. This is not to say that the nation has always been righteous in her behavior towards her neighbors, but it is to point out that the nation has not yet experienced the joy that is promised once they accept their Messiah. Israel's enemies have raged against her since the time Joshua conquered the Canaanites and will continue to do so right up to the Second Coming of Christ. In fact, Zechariah speaks of an invasion of the land right before the return of Christ. At that time Jerusalem will become "a cup that causes reeling to all the peoples around" (Zech 12:2). That is, the invading armies will become hysterical over their perceived opportunity of eradicating the Jews.

Contrary to the attitude of distain that has characterized Israel's enemies throughout her history, a time is coming when the nations that surround her will rejoice over her. The capital city will become "the joy of the whole earth" (Ps 48:2). God's plan is to make the city "a praise in the earth" (Isa 62:7). This of course presupposes a miraculous transformation of the hearts of the Gentile nations. God says, "behold, I create Jerusalem *for* rejoicing (Isa 65:19), then a bit later, "Then you will see *this*, and your heart will be glad" (Isa 66:14).

Jeremiah, prophesying at a time after Jerusalem had been devastated, projects a coming joyous day,

> It will be to Me a name of joy, praise, and glory before all the nations of the earth which will hear of all the good that I do for them, and they will fear and tremble because of all the good and all the peace that I make for it (Jer 33:9).

Jeremiah goes on to distinguish between a time when the city was lying desolate and a future day when it will be a center of great joy.

> Thus says the LORD, "Yet again there will be heard in this place, of which you say, 'It is a waste, without man and without beast,' *that is,* in the cities of Judah and in the streets of Jerusalem that are desolate, without man and without inhabitant and without beast, the voice of joy and the voice of gladness, the voice of the bridegroom and the voice of the bride, the voice of those who say, 'Give thanks to the Lord of hosts, for the Lord is good, for His lovingkindness is everlasting'; *and of those* who bring a thank offering into the house of the Lord. For I will restore the fortunes of the land as they were at first," says the Lord (Jer 33:10-11).

The prophet Zephaniah also looks forward to that day, "Shout for joy, O daughter of Zion! Shout *in triumph*, O Israel!

Rejoice and exult with all *your* heart, O daughter of Jerusalem!" When will this time of joy come? Zephaniah tells us that it will be when "the King of Israel, the Lord, is in your midst" (Zeph 3:14-15). Christ was in her midst at his First Coming, but the city did not rejoice at that time, but they will rejoice when they say, "Blessed is He who comes in the name of the Lord," that is, when they welcome Christ's return to rule the earth (Ps 118:26; Matt 23:39).

WORLD PEACE

The longing of the human heart throughout the centuries and over the millennia, has been for the absence of war and the presence of peace among the nations. From the battle of the five kings of Mesopotamia against the four kings of the Levant (Gen 14) to the final battle of Armageddon (Rev 19) human history has not known any lengthy period of peace. But several prophets reveal the millennial kingdom will be an unprecedented time of peace and prosperity. The Bible points to a time when Jerusalem will not only be filled with joyful people, but those nations around her will be at peace with her. In fact, Isaiah characterizes the Messiah as the "Prince of peace" and his government as one of "peace" (Isa 9:6-7).

> And He will judge between the nations, and will render decisions for many peoples; and they will hammer their swords into plowshares and their spears into pruning hooks. Nation will not lift up sword against nation, and never again will they learn war (Isa 2:4).

Micah states this same future condition using almost the exact same words,

> And He will judge between many peoples and render decisions for mighty, distant nations. Then they will ham-

mer their swords into plowshares and their spears into pruning hooks; nation will not lift up sword against nation, and never again will they train for war (Mic 4:3).

The prophet Hosea also sees this as a new period of unprecedented peace, "And I will abolish the bow, the sword and war from the land, and will make them lie down in safety" (Hos 2:18).

Zechariah makes clear this new peace will be worldwide, "And the bow of war will be cut off. And He will speak peace to the nations; and His dominion will be from sea to sea, and from the River to the ends of the earth (Zech 9:10).

A few chapters later, Zechariah says "There will no longer be a curse, for Jerusalem will dwell in security" (Zech 14:11). He is not referring to the lifting of the curse on the earth that came as a result of the fall of man into sin, for that will not be reversed until the eternal state (cf. Gen 3:17; Rev 22:3). Zechariah uses the term "curse" (*Herem*) to refer to certain things designated for judgment or total destruction. The prophet means that God will no longer designate Jerusalem for destruction by foreign armies.

At the conclusion of war in the Day of the Lord, Ezekiel notes that the weapons will be burned (Ezek 39:9-10). Why not keep the weapons for the next battle? Because they have come to the period of human history that will experience the end of wars.

Never in the history of the world has there been an extended period of peace, but when Christ rules on earth there will be peace among the nations.

ISRAEL LOVED AND HONORED BY HER NEIGHBORS

Many take offense to the notion that Israel will have a special role among the nations during the millennium. This is seen by some as an extreme form of Zionism. Yet, the Bible unabashedly says there will be a role reversal in the sense that Jerusalem and Israel, once at the bottom of the heap dominated by Gentile nations, will be granted a leading role in the Messiah's kingdom. This will not be due to her own goodness but due to the purpose God has for the nation.

The new world order brought about by the reign of Christ on earth will involve a reversal of Israel's fate, "They will take their captors captive and will rule over their oppressors" (Isa 14:2). But we must also keep in mind that those oppressors in the day Jeremiah calls the "time of Jacob's distress" will have enslaved the Israelites (Jer 30:7). But God will deliver them from the horrific persecution, "And strangers will no longer make them their slaves" (Jer 30:8). In a certain sense "the last shall be first." The most hated nation on earth will take on a new leadership role. But the Scripture makes it clear that Israel's leadership will not be vindictive in nature but rather benevolent. Isaiah says, she will be a "praise of all the earth" (Isa 62:7) and a blessing to the world,

> In the days to come Jacob will take root, Israel will blossom and sprout, and they will fill the whole world with fruit (Isa 27:6).

God first choose Israel to be "a kingdom of priests and a holy nation" at the Exodus (Exod 19:6). This means she was to be a vehicle of revelation to the nations and a mediator between the nations and God. Because of the nation's sin, Israel never successfully fulfilled this role. But in the millennium God will finally bring it to pass, "But you will be called the priests of the LORD; you will be spoken of *as* ministers of our God" (Isa 61:6). God does this first, by returning the nation to its land,

> Thus says the LORD of hosts, "Behold, I am going to save My people from the land of the east and from the land of the west; and I will bring them *back* and they will live in the midst of Jerusalem; and they shall be My people, and I will be their God in truth and righteousness" (Zech 8:7-8).

Perhaps the most surprising transformation will be in the hearts of the Gentile nations who once hated Israel. They will bless Israel, and Israel will bless them (Gen 12:3). They will love Israel's Messiah and his people. There will be a genuine heart-felt spiritual transformation in the attitude of the Gentile nations towards Israel.

> So the nations will fear the name of the LORD and all the kings of the earth Your glory. For the Lord has built up Zion; he has appeared in His glory (Ps 102:15-16).

> "At that time I will bring you in, even at the time when I gather you together; indeed, I will give you renown and praise among all the peoples of the earth, when I restore your fortunes before your eyes," says the Lord (Zeph 3:20).

This new reality in which the Gentiles honor Israel is perhaps most clearly seen when they aid the Jews in returning them from foreign lands to their homeland,

> Thus says the Lord GOD, "Behold, I will lift up My hand to the nations and set up My standard to the peoples; and they will bring your sons in *their* bosom, and your daughters will be carried on *their* shoulders. Kings will be your guardians, and their princesses your nurses. They will bow down to you with their faces to the earth" (Isa 49:22-23).

> Lift up your eyes round about and see; They all gather together, they come to you. Your sons will come from afar, and your daughters will be carried in the arms (Isa 60:4).

Foreign nations will also help Israel rebuild, "Foreigners will build up your walls, and their kings will minister to you" (Isa 60:10). Two great nations, Egypt and Assyria, which were former enemies of Israel, will love Israel and worship her God. First, Isaiah speaks about Egypt,

In that day five cities in the land of Egypt will be speaking the language of Canaan and swearing *allegiance* to the LORD of hosts; one will be called the City of Destruction. In that day there will be an altar to the LORD in the midst of the land of Egypt, and a pillar to the LORD near its border. It will become a sign and a witness to the LORD of hosts in the land of Egypt; for they will cry to the LORD because of oppressors, and He will send them a Savior and a Champion, and He will deliver them. Thus the LORD will make Himself known to Egypt, and the Egyptians will know the LORD in that day. They will even worship with sacrifice and offering, and will make a vow to the LORD and perform it. The LORD will strike Egypt, striking but healing; so they will return to the LORD, and He will respond to them and will heal them (Isa 19:18-22).

Isaiah goes on to reveal that not only Egypt but also the dreaded enemy Assyria will come to know Israel's God and worship him together with Egypt and Israel.

In that day there will be a highway from Egypt to Assyria, and the Assyrians will come into Egypt and the Egyptians into Assyria, and the Egyptians will worship with the Assyrians. In that day Israel will be the third *party* with Egypt and Assyria, a blessing in the midst of the earth, whom the LORD of hosts has blessed, saying, "Blessed is Egypt My people, and Assyria the work of My hands, and Israel My inheritance" (Isa 19:23-25).

Not only Egypt and Assyria but also nations from all over the world will come to Jerusalem to participate in the millennial worship. The Jewish people will be honored for their special relationship to God,

Thus says the LORD of hosts, "*It will* yet *be* that peoples will come, even the inhabitants of many cities. The inhabitants of one will go to another, saying, 'Let us go at once to entreat the favor of the LORD, and to seek the LORD of hosts; I will also go.' So many peoples and mighty nations will come to seek the LORD of hosts in Jerusalem and to entreat the favor of the LORD." Thus says the LORD of hosts, "In those days ten men from all the nations will grasp the garment of a Jew, saying, 'Let us go with you, for we have heard that God is with you'" (Zech 8:20-23).

This will be a miraculous (spiritual) transformation in the attitude of the Gentile nations towards Israel—the Jew once hated now loved.

WORLD COMMERCE: JERUSALEM'S SPECIAL ROLE

The ungodly city of Babylon will become the center of trade, idolatry, and persecution at the end of this age (Rev 17–18). But in contrast to her, after the return of Christ, Jerusalem will become the new locus of world commerce. In the following passages, notice how often the "wealth of the nations" is cited as now coming to Israel.

Then you will see and be radiant, and your heart will thrill and rejoice; because the abundance of the sea will be turned to you, the *wealth of the nations* will come to you (Isa 60:5)

For thus says the LORD of hosts, "Once more in a little while, I am going to shake the heavens and the earth, the sea also and the dry land. I will shake all the nations; and they will come with the wealth of all nations, and I will fill this house with glory," says the LORD of hosts.

"The silver is Mine and the gold is Mine," declares the LORD of hosts. "The latter glory of this house will be greater than the former," says the LORD of hosts, "and in this place I will give peace," declares the LORD of hosts (Hag 2:6-7).

Your gates will be open continually; they will not be closed day or night, so that *men* may bring to you *the wealth of the nations*, with their kings led in procession (Isa 60:11)

The above passage could not be referring to a condition in the new heaven and earth because at that time there will be no "night" (cf. Isa 60:11; Rev 21:25; 22:5). In the millennial setting Israel will finally live out her calling to be priests to God,

But you will be called the priests of the LORD; you will be spoken of *as* ministers of our God. You will eat the *wealth of nations*, and in their riches you will boast. Instead of your shame *you will have a* double *portion*, and *instead of* humiliation they will shout for joy over their portion. Therefore they will possess a double *portion* in their land, everlasting joy will be theirs (cf. Exod 19:6; Isa 61:6-7).

Nations will trade with Israel and Israel with the nations. Within Israel, God's people "will build houses and inhabit *them*; they will also plant vineyards and eat their fruit" (Isa 65:21). Jeremiah confirms this, "Again you will plant vineyards on the hills of Samaria; the planters will plant and will enjoy *them*" (Jer 31:5).

In view of these verses and Christ's rule of the world, we can assume unemployment will be a thing of the past. There will be abundance. A man and/or woman's labor will provide adequately for their needs so that there is no idleness, hunger, nor lack. Because of the improved climate (see below), and removal of famines and droughts, there will be productive agricultural work, managing of livestock, manufacturing, and trading of goods and services.

The unique role Israel will have in world commerce is not portrayed as something evil, but rather it will be a system of joy and honor, with God as the object of worship for the whole world.

CHAPTER 11

SPIRITUAL CONDITIONS IN THE KINGDOM

THE WORSHIP AND RULE OF ONLY ONE GOD IN THE WORLD

The Second Coming will inaugurate a major change in God's administration of the peoples of the entire world. One of the most phenomenal realities of the millennial kingdom will be the fact that there will be no more idolatry, worship of idols or false religions in the entire world. Christ alone will be the focus of millennial worship.

Perhaps more succinctly than any other prophet, Zechariah clarifies this truth:

And the LORD will be king over all the earth; in that day the LORD will be the only one, and His name the only one (Zech 14:9).

Isaiah prophesied this same vision of God's rule as did the Apostle John (Isa 37:16; 45:5-6, 14, 18, 22; 46:9; Zech 14:9; Rev

125

20:6). The term "one" in Zechariah 14:9 denotes the idea that Yahweh has become the solitary, unique God of the entire world (cf. Ps 22:27; 86:9; Isa 66:23; Rev 15:4).

The result will be that the nations of the earth will now worship the one true God,

> "Many nations will join themselves to the LORD in that day and will become My people. Then I will dwell in your midst, and you will know that the LORD of hosts has sent Me to you (Zech 2:11).

Zechariah also notes that all forms of idolatry will be terminated,

> "It will come about in that day," declares the LORD of hosts, "that I will cut off the names of the idols from the land, and they will no longer be remembered; and I will also remove the prophets and the unclean spirit from the land" (Zech 13:2).

Idolatry, which comprises the worship of a multitude of gods and which the Apostle Paul noted as demonically inspired, will be cut off and non-existent (1 Cor 10:20; Zech 13:2; Rev 20:1-3). Hosea also refers to this new condition, "For I will remove the names of the Baals from her mouth, so that they will be mentioned by their names no more" (Hos 2:17). The Apostle John refers to this worldwide adoration just prior to Christ's coming when he states, "Who will not fear, O Lord, and glorify Thy name" (Rev 15:4).

Ezekiel refers to this removal of idolatry from a spiritual standpoint, "Then I will sprinkle clean water on you, and you will be clean; I will cleanse you from all your filthiness and from all your idols…They will no longer defile themselves with their idols, or with their detestable things, or with any of their transgressions" (Ezek 36:25; 37:23).

This is truly phenomenal when we consider the plethora of gods worshiped across the globe. Zechariah asserts that there will be just one God. Yahweh will be the object of worship not just of Israel but of the entire the earth (cf. Zech 2:15; 8:20-23).

The unity of God revealed in Israel's Shema, "Hear O Israel! The Lord our God, the Lord is one," was only true for Israel as God's chosen people and those who identified with Israel's God, but now it is expanded to become the declaration of every nation on the face of "all the earth" (cf. Deut 6:4; Zech 14:9).

This will be a new and absolutely unique development in world history. Nothing even close to it has taken place since the fall, though the Bible often alludes to it (Ps 93:1; 96:9-10; 97:1-9; 99:1-5; Jer 3:17). It is difficult if not impossible to ascribe this condition to the church in the present age. In addition, the concluding verses of Zechariah where nations are judged for refusing to worship God, make this designation difficult to harmonize with the eternal state. Zechariah has made clear that Yahweh's rule is yet to come to earth in a way never-before experienced, fulfilling the prayer of Matthew 6:10, "Your kingdom come. Your will be done, on earth as it is in heaven."

KNOWLEDGE OF GOD

The judgments that precede and accompany the Second Coming of Christ, will eradicate all those who are opposed to God's rule on the earth (Matt 13:30, 36-43, 47-50; 25:31-46). Thus, at the beginning of the millennial kingdom all those (Jews and Gentiles) who enter it shall know the Lord. Isaiah reveals that the knowledge of God will be universal,

> They will not hurt or destroy in all My holy mountain, for the earth will be full of the knowledge of the LORD as the waters cover the sea (Isa 11:9).

Habakkuk declares the same message, "For the earth will be filled with the knowledge of the glory of the LORD, as the waters cover the sea" (Hab 2:14).

Jeremiah states in his passage on the New Covenant, "They will not teach again, each man his neighbor and each man his brother, saying, 'Know the LORD,' for they will all know Me, from the least of them to the greatest of them," declares the LORD, "for I will forgive their iniquity, and their sin I will remember no more" (Jer 31:34).

Though all shall know the Lord throughout the millennium, at the end of it, Satan will be loosed for a short period and lead one final rebellion that will involve a multitude of people, as many as "the sand of the seashore" (Rev 20:7-8). Thus, during the thousand-year period many new generations will arise, and the children born will need to come to faith in the Messiah. Though most will believe in the Messiah, some will not. Although the knowledge of the Lord will cover the whole earth during the millennium, after many generations, apparently at the very end after Satan is released, a rebellion against God will mount, demonstrating that even in an almost idyllic world, the Adamic nature at its core is in rebellion against God and unless called to faith and repentance will rebel. However, with regard to the nation of Israel, there are a few passages that seem to indicate that the nation once converted to the Messiah will never again rebel. If that is the case, then the rebellion after the thousand years will most likely come from the Gentile peoples that have repopulated the earth.

A KINGDOM ON EARTH CHARACTERIZED BY HOLINESS

Some who object to the notion of a millennial kingdom do so because the very idea is that it occurs on this fallen earth, thus, it is an *earthly* kingdom. They equate it with a lack of spirituality.

This is diametrically opposed to what the Scriptures teach about the millennial kingdom.

> For then I will give to the peoples purified lips, that all of them may call on the name of the LORD (Zeph 3:9).

> In that day the Branch of the LORD will be beautiful and glorious, and the fruit of the earth *will be* the pride and the adornment of the survivors of Israel. It will come about that he who is left in Zion and remains in Jerusalem will be called holy—everyone who is recorded for life in Jerusalem. When the Lord has washed away the filth of the daughters of Zion and purged the bloodshed of Jerusalem from her midst, by the spirit of judgment and the spirit of burning (Isa 4:2-4).

> And they will call them, "The holy people, the redeemed of the LORD"; and you will be called, "Sought out, a city not forsaken" (Isa 63:12).

When Ezekiel summarizes Israel's conversion and return to the land, he emphasizes the entirely new life of holiness that they will live,

> "For I will take you from the nations, gather you from all the lands and bring you into your own land. Then I will sprinkle clean water on you, and you will be clean; I will cleanse you from all your filthiness and from all your idols. Moreover, I will give you a new heart and put a new spirit within you; and I will remove the heart of stone from your flesh and give you a heart of flesh. I will put My Spirit within you and cause you to walk in My statutes, and you will be careful to observe My ordinances. You will live in the land that I gave to your forefathers; so you will be My people, and I will be your God" (Ezek 36:24-28).

129

Those returning to Israel at that time will have been cleansed of their sin, "A highway will be there, a roadway, and it will be called the Highway of Holiness. The unclean will not travel on it, but it *will* be for him who walks *that* way, and fools will not wander *on it*" (Isa 60:8). In fact, even such mundane things as bells on a horse or cooking ware will be set apart to God,

> In that day there will *be inscribed* on the bells of the horses, "Holy to the Lord." And the cooking pots in the Lord's house will be like the bowls before the altar. Every cooking pot in Jerusalem and in Judah will be holy to the Lord of hosts (Zech 14:20-21).

Thus, the kingdom is earthly in the sense that it is on the earth, but holiness will characterize it.

TEMPLE WORSHIP (IN THE SPIRIT) RESTORED IN JERUSALEM

I dealt earlier with some of the objections to the idea that a millennial temple will be built, so I will not defend the idea here, except to say there is abundant revelation that clearly points to a millennial temple in Jerusalem.[9] In the last passage cited above, Zechariah alludes to the temple when he refers to the "altar," presumably the altar where burnt offerings are made. The altar is a piece of the temple furniture (Zech 14:20).

Zechariah also reveals that it is the "Branch," a term for the Messiah, who will build the millennial temple (cf. Jer 23:5; 33:15; Zech 3:8),

> Thus says the LORD of hosts, "Behold, a man whose name is Branch, for He will branch out from where He is; and He will build the temple of the LORD. Yes, it

---

9   Ezekiel's millennial temple is not to be confused with the possible rebuilding of the temple in the Day of the Lord which precedes the millennial state (2 Thess 2:1-4; Rev 11:1-2).

is He who will build the temple of the LORD, and He who will bear the honor and sit and rule on His throne. Thus, He will be a priest on His throne, and the counsel of peace will be between the two offices" (Zech 6:12-13).

Isaiah prophesies about this future temple in Zion,

Now it will come about that in the last days the mountain of the house of the LORD will be established as the chief of the mountains, and will be raised above the hills; and all the nations will stream to it. And many peoples will come and say, "Come, let us go up to the mountain of the LORD, to the house of the God of Jacob; that He may teach us concerning His ways and that we may walk in His paths." For the law will go forth from Zion and the word of the LORD from Jerusalem (Isa 2:2-3).

It is not just Isaiah and Zechariah who prophesy of a future temple, the prophet Micah quotes this passage from Isaiah almost verbatim (Mic 4:1-2).

The prophet Haggai is not so specific, but he does refer to a future time when the glory of God's house (the temple) will supersede even the glory of Solomon's temple:

For thus says the LORD of hosts, "Once more in a little while, I am going to shake the heavens and the earth, the sea also and the dry land. I will shake all the nations; and they will come with the wealth of all nations, and I will fill this house with glory," says the LORD of hosts. "The silver is Mine and the gold is Mine," declares the LORD of hosts. "The latter glory of this house will be greater than the former," says the LORD of hosts, "and in this place I will give peace," declares the LORD of hosts (Hag 2:6-9).

Also, the prophet Malachi foresees a day when the Messiah will enter into his temple. Many think this prophecy refers to an event during Christ's First Advent, but it more accurately describes his Second Coming in judgment,

> The Lord, whom you seek, will suddenly come to His temple; and the messenger of the covenant, in whom you delight, behold, He is coming, says the LORD of hosts, but who can endure the day of His coming? And who can stand when He appears? For He is like a refiner's fire and like fullers' soap. He will sit as a smelter and purifier of silver (Mal 3:1-3).

It is prophet Ezekiel that gives the most astounding and detailed revelation of this new temple. The temple he envisions, with its detailed measurements, sacrificial and priestly duties, has never been built in the long history of Israel (Ezek 40–42). Nor does his temple equate with the measurements of the New Jerusalem (Rev 21:15-17). Because of this, many theologians prefer to see it as an allegorical or symbolic rendition of the so-called ideal temple, but there is nothing in the account of Ezekiel 40–48 to lead us to an allegorical or symbolic interpretation. If it is taken at its face value as described, we must assume Ezekiel's temple has never been built, yet will be erected at a future time. Most likely it is a vision of the millennial temple.

The Old Testament prophets witness to a future ministry of Levitical priests in the millennial temple. Jeremiah maintains that the revival of the Levitical priesthood is as assured as the revival of the Davidic throne,

> For thus says the LORD, "David shall never lack a man to sit on the throne of the house of Israel; And the Levitical priests shall never lack a man before Me to offer burnt offerings, to burn grain offerings and to prepare sacrifices continually" (Jer 33:18).

Ezekiel's account maintains that the reinstituted priesthood will come from the line of Zadok who descended through Levi. When describing the priest chambers in the new temple, he states:

> but the chamber which faces toward the north is for the priests who keep charge of the altar. These are the sons of Zadok, who from the sons of Levi come near to the LORD to minister to Him (Ezek 40:46).

Zadok was a family line of the Levitical priesthood that remained faithful when other priests and Levites went into apostasy.

Malachi says God will purify the Levites in preparation for millennial worship, "He will sit as a smelter and purifier of silver, and He will purify the sons of Levi and refine them like gold and silver, so that they may present to the LORD offerings in righteousness" (Mal 3:3). We do not know which Jews still scattered abroad in the diaspora might be of Levitical lineage, but God does (Isa 60:20-21). Ezekiel is quite specific in noting that the Levitical priests who will serve in the future temple will be of the family line of Zadok (Ezek 40:46; 43:19; 44:15; 48:11).

Jews worshipping at the millennial temple will offer animal sacrifices (Isa 19:21; 56:6-7; Hag 2:7). The prophets Jeremiah and Ezekiel specify sacrifices of bulls, rams, goats, and lambs, for burnt offerings, peace offerings, sin offerings, guilt offerings, grain and meal offerings (Jer 33:17-18; Ezek 40:38-42; 42:13; 43:18-21-25; 44:11,15; 23; 45:13-17; 46:2, 4,11-12, 24).

Doubtless, these offerings will reflect the Messiah's all-sufficient sacrifice (Heb 9:24-26; 10:11-12). Certain millennial sacrifices are said to make atonement for the altar (Ezek 43:20, 26), for the house of Israel (45:15, 17), and for the temple (Ezek 45:20). They will probably effect "atonement" in a similar way as the Levitical sacrifices under the Old Covenant also procured temporal atonement for specific sins (Lev 4:20, 35; 16:27; 17:11). Just as the "atonement" procured in the sacrificial system under the Old Covenant was ultimately based upon the death of the Messiah, so too will the "atonement" of these millennial sacrifices will be based on Christ's death and serve as a memorial to it. However, they will take place under the New Covenant. Whereas under the Mosaic Law the animal sacrifices pointed forward to the coming Messiah and effected a temporary atonement for designated sins (e.g. Lev 1:4; 4:20, etc.), in the Millennium, sacrifices under the New Covenant will point backwards to commemorate aspects of Christ's supreme (and finished) sacrifice.

In addition, certain holy days, or festivals such as the Sabbath, the new moons, the Feast of Booths, the feast of Passover and Unleavened Bread will be celebrated in Israel under the New Covenant with renewed significance (Isa 56:6; Ezek 44:24; 45:17-25; 46:3, 12; Zech 14:16-19, 21). Jeremiah said regarding the New Covenant, "I will put my law within them and on their heart" (Jer 31:31, 33). So, though these sacrifices and festivals are similar to those instituted by Moses, they will be celebrated in a new and spiritual way that pleases God, and under the New Covenant.

The new temple will not only be a new focus of worship for the Jews, but also Gentiles will travel from all parts of the globe to worship Christ in Jerusalem,

> All nations whom You have made shall come and worship before You, O Lord, and they shall glorify Your name (Ps 86:9).

> Worship the LORD in holy attire; tremble before Him, all the earth. Say among the nations, "The LORD reigns"; Indeed, the world is firmly established, it will not be moved; He will judge the peoples with equity (Ps 96:9-10).

Also, the foreigners who join themselves to the LORD, to minister to Him, and to love the name of the LORD, to be His servants, everyone who keeps from profaning the sabbath and holds fast My covenant; even those I will bring to My holy mountain and make them joyful in My house of prayer. Their burnt offerings and their sacrifices will be acceptable on My altar; for My house will be called a house of prayer for all the peoples. (Isa 56:6-7).

This center of worship in Jerusalem will in no way abrogate the personal worship of the heart, "in spirit and truth" that will take place anywhere at any time (John 4:21-24). One advancement in worship that the millennial believer will have over that experienced by the church today, is that as well as being able to worship God "in spirit and truth" and through the Spirit, they will be able to witness a physical manifestation of God's glory in Jerusalem at the temple when they journey there to participate in worship.

CHAPTER 12

FULFILLMENT OF THE MAJOR BIBLICAL COVENANTS

FULFILLMENT OF THE ABRAHAMIC COVENANT

The Abrahamic Covenant is in some ways the most important covenant in the Old Testament. I say this because it forms the basis of the Davidic and New Covenants. Though there are seven statements of promise made to Abraham in Genesis 12:1-3, I summarized these promises earlier as: (1) land (2) a great nation of descendants, and (3) blessing. Multiple times in the book of Genesis God promised Abraham a land (with borders specified), innumerable descendants, and blessing (Gen 12:1-3; 13:14-17, 15:3-5, 18; 17:7-8). Though these promises were partially fulfilled historically, their full and final fulfillment awaits the reign of the Messiah. In their fulfillment, I would like to consider these from a fourfold perspective.

1. *The Promise of Descendants*

God began to fulfill His promise to give Abraham many descendants with the birth of Isaac (Gen 21:1). By the time of the Exodus, the Abrahamic family had multiplied exceedingly so that the Egyptians began to fear them, "But the more they afflicted them, the more they multiplied and the more they spread out, so that they were in dread of the sons of Israel…God was good to the midwives, and the people multiplied, and became very mighty" (Exod 1:12, 20). By the time of King Solomon, Scripture reveals to us, "Judah and Israel were as numerous as the sand that is on the seashore in abundance; they were eating and drinking and rejoicing" (1 Kgs 4:20).

Still, prophetic scriptures reveal that in the millennial era, God will multiply Abraham's descendants even more,

> And the days of your mourning will be over. Then all your people *will be* righteous; They will possess the land forever, the branch of My planting, the work of My hands, that I may be glorified. The smallest one will become a clan, and the least one a mighty nation. I, the LORD, will hasten it in its time." (Isa 60:20-22).

> I will multiply men on you, all the house of Israel, all of it; and the cities will be inhabited and the waste places will be rebuilt. I will multiply on you man and beast; and they will increase and be fruitful; and I will cause you to be inhabited as you were formerly and will treat you better than at the first. Thus you will know that I am the LORD (Ezek 36:10-11).

> I will make a covenant of peace with them; it will be an everlasting covenant with them. And I will place them and multiply them, and will set My sanctuary in their midst forever (Ezek 37:26).

This aspect of the promise still awaits a future fulfillment. Moses foresees a future day when the nation will turn in faith to God (something that has not yet happened in the history of Israel), and God will bless and multiply them.

"The LORD your God will bring you into the land which your fathers possessed, and you shall possess it; and He will prosper you and multiply you more than your fathers (Deut 30:6).

2. The Promise of the Land

A second major aspect of the Abrahamic covenant was the land grant, which has been—to say the least—a bone of contention to this day. The passages just cited above that mention descendants also mention that Israel will finally have full possession of her promised land. Several Scriptures delineate the general borders of the promised land (Gen 12:7; 13:14-15; 15:18-21; Exod 23:31; Num13:21; Deut 11:24; 1 Kgs 8:65; 2 Kgs14:25; Isa 27:12), and a couple other passages give its specific boundary lines (Num 34:1-14; Josh 15–19). In all of Israel's history, the nation has never possessed the land of promise to the full extent of its promised borders.

Joshua and the author of Judges both clarify that Israel fell short of driving the Canaanites out of the land in most all the tribes (Josh 16:10; 17:12; Judg 1:27–2:3). As of this present time, Israel has returned to her land, but only partially. Although many Jews have returned to the land, it is estimated that even today the majority of Jewish people still live outside the land of Israel. Those living in the land still face constant harassment from neighboring people (this is not to deny that unconverted Israel is sometimes unrighteous in her dealings with those neighbors).

The largest land territory that Israel controlled in the nation's history was at the highpoint of the kingdom under David and Solomon, and yet even then it fell short of the borders given in some of the Scriptures cited above. The Abrahamic covenant promised an uninterrupted possession of the land by Abraham's descendants. That has never been experienced by the nation. It is the prophet Ezekiel who delineates the borders of the tribes of Israel in the millennial kingdom (Ezek 47:13-21; 48:1-28). Israel will finally live within the promised borders at that time when the Messiah rules.

Though many argue that Israel has at times unjustly taken control of some of the land, it must be remembered that the land of Israel itself, as well as the whole earth, belongs to God its creator (Gen 1:1; Ps 24:1; Exod 19:5; Lev 25:23; Deut 10:14). As the Supreme Sovereign, he has the right to distribute it as he wills. The land was granted to Israel as a gift. Through disobedience they have in the past forfeited the right to remain in the land, but those times of dispersion and discipline do not rescind the gift itself. At least twice in the nation's history, it was removed from their land, the Assyrian and Babylonian captivities, and the Roman invasion after the time of Christ. But the Apostle Paul emphasizes, "The gifts and the calling of God are irrevocable" (Rom 11:29).

God's gift of the land to Israel is "forever" (Gen 13:15). Some have argued that the term "forever" (*'olam*) is used in some contexts only to mean for a lifetime or an extended period of time. For example, in Exodus 21:6 a slave who pierces his ear becomes a permanent (*'olam*) servant. So the term there cannot mean forever, but rather for the duration of the slave's life. Another example is Isaiah 9:7, "There will be no end to the increase of *His* government or of peace, on the throne of David and over his kingdom, to establish it and to uphold it with justice and righteousness from then on and *forevermore* (*'olam*). If the millennium lasts only a thousand years (as stated six times in Rev 20:1-7), then how can it be said that Christ will rule on the throne of David forever? There are two plausible answers. One is that in this context "forever" means for a long duration, the duration of the millennium. Or probably more plausible as I delineated earlier is the view that Christ's millennial reign will transition seamlessly into eternity. What began in the millennium will continue on into the eternal state. Christ's reign will begin on earth at the start of the millennium but then will continue into the new heaven and earth. In that sense, it is forever.

However, it is also important to point out that the term "forever" (*'olam*), can mean eternal. For example, the term is employed to describe God's existence, "But the LORD abides forever" (Ps 9:7). This usage can hardly mean a temporary duration. Examples abound in the Old Testament where the term *'olam* means forever, "Blessed be the LORD, the God of Israel, from everlasting even to everlasting" (1 Chron 16:36). Or "Before the mountains were born or You gave birth to the earth and the world, even from everlasting to everlasting, You are God" (Ps 90:2). In these last two examples the Hebrew term *'olam* is used twice and translated as "from everlasting to everlasting." The double use of the word in Hebrew, "forever and ever," gives the phrase an intensive meaning. This double use is employed by Jeremiah when referring to the land gift, "then I will let you dwell in this place, in the land that I gave to your fathers forever and ever," and again later in his book, "dwell on the land which the LORD has given to you and your forefathers forever and ever" (Jer 7:7; 25:5). So, the context must guide us when interpreting the Hebrew word "forever."

The land grant remains valid and irrevocable even in spite of Israel's unbelief and rejection of her Messiah (Rom 9:3-5; 11:28-29). Psalm 105:8-11 makes this clear,

He has remembered His covenant forever, the word which He commanded to a thousand generations, *the covenant* which He made with Abraham, and His oath to

Isaac. Then He confirmed it to Jacob for a statute, to Israel as an everlasting covenant, saying, "To you I will give the land of Canaan as the portion of your inheritance."

However, the privilege of occupying the land at any particular period in history is contingent upon the nation's obedience and God's grace (Lev 26:27-33; Deut 30). Even in periods of discipline when the nation is driven outside the land, God has pledged himself to remain faithful to his promise of giving them the land (Lev 26:40-45; Deut 30:1-10). In fact, in Israel's end-time final repentance, God promises to bring Jews scattered across the world back to their homeland (Isa 60:4-14; Deut 30:1-5).

Lift up your eyes round about and see; they all gather together, they come to you. Your sons will come from afar, and your daughters will be carried in the arms. Then you will see and be radiant, and your heart will thrill and rejoice (Isa 60:4-5).

This final regathering of Jews to the land of Israel will not just be the Jews from Babylon and Persia but from all parts of the world, "gathered from the lands, from the east and from the west, from the north and from the south" (Ps 107:3). Ezekiel records the actual dispersing of the future millennial land allotments that are significantly different than any occupation in Israel's past history (Ezek 47:13–48:29).

3. The Promise of a Great Nation

It is noteworthy that from Genesis 12 through the rest of the Old Testament, in fact, including the Gospels in the New Testament, the writers' focus is on the historical development of a single people group, the nation of Israel. An aspect of the Abrahamic covenant was the promise to make Abraham's descendants into a great nation, "and I will make you a great nation" (Gen 12:3). One could argue that in the history of the nations of the world, none was quite so unique and distinct as Israel. Israel's uniqueness, however, is not due to its human accomplishments but rather to God's election and employment of the nation as his primary conduit through which he would reveal himself, his salvation, and his plan for the earth. He did this by entrusting them "with the oracles of God," the Scriptures (cf. Rom 3:2; 9:4-5).

Yet, to be frank and honest, most of their history has been spent in humiliation, facing hatred and enmity from the Gentiles. A time is coming, when this tiny little nation will be the pride of the nations of the world. In Psalm 2:8 God promises the Messiah that he will give to him the nations of the earth, "Ask of Me, and I will surely give the nations as Your inheritance, and the *very* ends of the earth as Your possession." But it will be a new relationship that is accompanied by great joy, "Beautiful in elevation, the joy of the whole earth, Is Mount Zion *in* the far north, the city of the great King." (Ps 48:2).

The nations will be not only reconciled to God but also to Israel, and Israel to the nations. At that time Israel will be so admired that to be born a Jew will be considered a high honor:

> But of Zion it shall be said, "This one and that one were born in her"; and the Most High Himself will establish her. The LORD will count when He registers the peoples, "this one was born there." *Selah*. Then those who sing as well as those who play the flutes *shall say*, "all my springs *of joy* are in you" (Ps 87:5-7).

> Then their offspring will be known among the nations, and their descendants in the midst of the peoples. All who see them will recognize them because they are the offspring *whom* the LORD has blessed (Isa 61:9).

In addition, Israel will be esteemed because it is the one nation in the world to which the nations will sojourn to learn more about God,

And many peoples will come and say, "Come, let us go up to the mountain of the LORD, to the house of the God of Jacob; that He may teach us concerning His ways and that we may walk in His paths." For the law will go forth from Zion and the word of the LORD from Jerusalem (Isa 2:3).

At the time of the millennium, Israel will truly be a great nation as never before in history. The prophet Isaiah waited eagerly for the day of Israel's greatness, "And give Him no rest until He establishes and makes Jerusalem a praise in the earth" (Isa 62:7)

4. The Promise of Blessing

From the time of the fall of Adam and Eve in the garden and the entrance of sin into the world, God intended once more to bring all mankind under the influence of His blessing which had been lost (Gen 3:15). Abraham was to be His primary instrument through which God would channel His blessing (Gen 12:3; 22:18; 26:4; 28:14). Under the Mosaic covenant God promised numerous temporal blessings if the nation were obedient (Deut 28:1-14), but the Abrahamic blessing was spiritual and eternal in nature and ultimately refers to the salvation that the Messiah would procure and grant to Israel. The Apostle Paul clarifies how this promise of blessing extended to the Gentiles—through their faith in the Messiah.

The Scripture, foreseeing that God would justify the Gentiles by faith, preached the gospel beforehand to Abraham, *saying*, "All the Nations will be blessed in you." So then those who are of faith are blessed with Abraham, the believer (Gal 3:8-9).

In Ephesians 2:12-13 Paul indicates that at one time Gentiles were cut off from God, "strangers to the covenants of promise," but in Christ they have been "brought near" indicating that they now share in the blessing of the eternal covenants originally made with Israel. Yet this is sharing with Israel not replacing her. The result is that at this present time Gentiles have equal access to God with Jewish believers, "For through Him we both have our access in one Spirit to the Father. So then you are no longer strangers and aliens, but you are fellow citizens with the saints, and are of God's household" (Eph 2:18-19).

This promise of blessing for Gentiles does not negate the promise of blessing to the ethnic Jews, for in Peter's Pentecost message he reminded the Jews that God's promise was still valid, "It is you who are the sons of the prophets and of the covenant which God made with your fathers, saying to Abraham, 'And in your seed all the families of the earth shall be blessed.' For you first, God raised up His Servant and sent Him to bless you by turning every one *of you* from your wicked ways" (Acts 3:25-26).

Although today Jewish believers in the Messiah along with Gentile believers form one body, the church (Eph 2:11-22), there remains yet the unfulfilled promise made to the physical seed (descendants) of Abraham, national Israel. In Romans 11:17-24, Paul employs the example of an olive tree to illustrate the difference between unbelieving national Israel, believing Gentiles (and Jews) in the church, and future belief by the nation of Israel.

In the illustration, the olive tree root probably represents God's sovereign election of the patriarchs, Abraham, Isaac, and Jacob to be the conduit of his salvation program. The natural branches of the olive tree were the Jews descended from the patriarchs. At the rejection of the Messiah, they were broken off from the olive tree root. This represents God's (temporary) decision to remove the nation of Israel from its official position as God's representatives and vehicle of revelation and salvation to the world (the remnant of Jews today who believe in Jesus are part of the body of Christ, the church). The wild branches that were then grafted into the olive tree root represent the Gentile

145

believers who come to faith in the Jewish Messiah who now are considered part of the church along with Jewish believers. But there remains the option for God to graft back into the olive tree root the natural branches that he broke off, that is, ethnic Israel. This points to a future period when the nation repents, receives her Messiah, and experiences the fulfillment of the Abrahamic promise.

In fact, Paul specifically says Israel has experienced a "partial hardening," partial because some Jews do believe in Jesus as the Messiah, but most do not. This will be the situation "until the fullness of Gentiles will come in" (Rom 11:25). Once that period is over, "all Israel will be saved." This refers to the conversion of national Israel, that is, those who embrace the Messiah in faith, as I wrote about previously. Paul goes on to say, "Just as it is written, 'the deliverer will come from Zion, he will remove ungodliness from Jacob'" (Rom 11:26). I quote the whole olive tree illustration below for your consideration:

> But if some of the branches were broken off (unbelieving Jews), and you, being a wild olive, were grafted in among them and became partaker with them of the rich root of the olive tree, do not be arrogant toward the branches; but if you are arrogant, remember that it is not you who supports the root, but the root supports you. You will say then, "Branches were broken off so that I might be grafted in." Quite right, they were broken off for their unbelief, but you stand by your faith. Do not be conceited, but fear; for if God did not spare the natural branches, He will not spare you, either. Behold then the kindness and severity of God; to those who fell, severity, but to you, God's kindness, if you continue in His kindness; otherwise you also will be cut off. And they also, if they do not continue in their unbelief, will be grafted in, for God is able to graft them in again. For if you were cut off

from what is by nature a wild olive tree, and were grafted contrary to nature into a cultivated olive tree, how much more will these who are the natural branches be grafted into their own olive tree? For I do not want you, brethren, to be uninformed of this mystery—so that you will not be wise in your own estimation—that a partial hardening has happened to Israel until the fullness of the Gentiles has come in; and so all Israel will be saved; just as it is written, "The Deliverer will come from Zion, He will remove ungodliness from Jacob" (Rom 11:17-24).

The blessing that we have experienced through faith Christ will be experienced by national ethnic Israel in the future. God will graft them back into to his elective purposes. The nation will experience the salvation-blessing that God promised to Abraham (Gen 12:2; 22:17).

THE MOSAIC COVENANT WAS FULFILLED—
BUT NOT REINSTATED

In the Sermon on the Mount, after Jesus clarified that He had not come to do away with the law but to fulfill it, He made this interesting comment, "For truly I say to you, until heaven and earth pass away, not the smallest letter or stroke shall pass from the Law until all is accomplished" (Matt 5:18). Because of this statement, we might be tempted to think that the Mosaic Law may not be completely fulfilled until the end of the millennium when the old heaven and earth pass away (Rev 21:1). This would leave room for the Mosaic Law to be in effect during the millennial era. However, Jesus may be using the term "Law" as a broader reference to the whole Old Testament for in the previous verse He referred to "the Law and the Prophets." If this is the case, then He would be saying that not all the law and all of prophecy would be fulfilled until the onset of the new heaven and earth (Matt 5:17). In this view, He would fulfill the Mosaic Law in His earthly life and death, but all prophecy would not be fulfilled until the end of the millennium and the beginning of the new heaven and earth. There is scriptural reason for believing that Jesus did fulfill the Mosaic law.

In quoting Jeremiah, the author of Hebrews states, "When He said, 'A new *covenant*,' He has made the first obsolete. But whatever is becoming obsolete and growing old is ready to disappear" (Heb 8:13). Although the writer says the old covenant (of which the law is a part) is "obsolete" and "ready to disappear," he does not definitively say it has disappeared. He may have expressed the point in that way if at the time of writing the temple was still standing in Jerusalem and sacrifices were still being offered—before the Roman invasion and destruction of the temple in AD 70. However, the Apostle Paul seems to indicate that the law had served its temporal purpose,

> Why the Law then? It was added because of transgressions, having been ordained through angels by the agency of a mediator, until the seed would come to whom the promise had been made...But before faith came, we were kept in custody under the law, being shut up to the faith which was later to be revealed. Therefore, the Law has become our tutor *to lead us* to Christ, so that we may be justified by faith. But now that faith has come, we are no longer under a tutor (Gal 3:19, 23-25).

"We are no longer under a tutor," that is we are no longer under the Mosaic Law. If Jesus fulfilled the Law through his life, death, and resurrection, then why do laws and festivals show up again in millennial economy? Although there are similarities between the millennial sacrifices and festivals and the Mosaic sacrifices and festivals, there are also many differences so that it is not necessary to argue that Israel will be placed back under the Mosaic Covenant.

There are several ways in which millennial worship will differ from worship under the Mosaic Covenant. Probably the most significant difference will be the operation of the Spirit among the Israelites in the New Covenant economy. The millennial temple is significantly different in proportion and measurements to all previous temples in Jerusalem. From the revelation Ezekiel has given regarding the millennial temple, there is no mention of the Ark of the Covenant, no tablets of stone, no curtains with cherubim, no separating veil, no high priest, no evening sacrifice. There is an altar of burnt offering, but the measurements differ from the bronze altar of the Mosaic period. There is no mention of the Feast of Pentecost, Feast of Trumpets, nor Day of Atonement, but there is mention of a new year's festival that did not exist under the Mosaic Law (Ezek 45:18-20). There is no lampstand and no showbread. Also, in contrast to the Mosaic period only Levitical priests from the line of Zadok may serve in offering sacrifices (Ezek 40:46; 43:19: 44:15-31). In addition, instead of forty-eight Levitical cities, the priests and Levites will dwell in a specified land area (cf. Num 35:1-8; Ezek 45:3-5). But there will be God's throne in the millennial temple, whereas in the temple built by Solomon, God was said to dwell above and between the cherubim which were part of the Ark of the Covenant (Ezek 43:4-8). So, although there are several similarities to Old Testament feasts and sacrifices, there are also many differences.

The first Lord's Supper that the disciples celebrated with Jesus was the Jewish Passover. From our perspective, it was both a Passover and the newly initiated Lord's Supper. After that, whenever the Lord's Supper was celebrated by the church there were both differences and similarities with the Jewish Passover. In like manner, there are also similarities and differences between the Mosaic sacrifices and feasts and the millennial sacrifices and feasts. It is perhaps helpful to note that the millennial sacrifices and feasts are never called "Mosaic" sacrifices or feasts by the biblical writers.

So, in summary, several millennial sacrifices and feasts are similar to Mosaic sacrifices and feasts, and yet they are also distinct, so that we need not believe that the Mosaic Law will be reinstituted during the millennium.

FULFILLMENT OF THE PALESTINIAN COVENANT

Not many theologians recognize the Palestinian Covenant as a separate compact from the Mosaic Covenant. Yet it is worth pointing out how this covenant supplements the Mosaic agreement. The Palestinian covenant takes its modern name from the ancient reference to the land of Israel as Palestine. The covenant was made with Israel prior to the nation's entrance into the land of Canaan—some thirty-nine years after the Mosaic covenant was made at Mount Sinai. Israel was positioned on the border of the promised land. The agreement consisted of curses and blessings. In general, if Israel remained obedient, God would grant them temporal blessing in the world (Deut 28:1-14; 30:1-20), but if they were disobedient God would bring temporal curses upon them in the form of judgments (Deut 27:11-26; 28:15-68; 29:22-28). In Israel's history the nation did experience both the judgments and the blessings contained in the covenant. Noteworthy is the fact that this addendum to Mosaic covenant foresees a future day when the nation, scattered across the world, will repent and turn to the Lord (Deut 30:1-6). In that future turning to God, the Lord will grant to them a new heart promised in the New Covenant (cf. Deut 30:6; Jer 31:33). Then they will fully experience the blessings (both temporal and eternal) promised in all her covenants.

FULFILLMENT OF THE DAVIDIC COVENANT

The monarchy in Israel was always part of God's plan reaching back to the promise made to Abraham that kings would descend from him. It began with Saul who was selected by God as a concession to the request of the people (I Sam 9:15–17; 10:1, 10; 15:17). Saul's blatant disobedience disqualified him to be the person through whom God would mediate his covenant rule (1 Sam 13:8–14; 15:1-29). God then chose David and his descendants to begin a line of kings that would extend to the Messiah (I Sam 16:1, 11-13; 2 Sam 7:8, 12, 16).

The Davidic Covenant comprises the most detailed disclosure on the Messianic rule in the Old Testament. When this revelation is compared with the promise made in Luke 1 to Mary, the mother of Jesus, it becomes clear that Jesus is the promised king to rule forever on David's throne (2 Sam 7:8-16; Luke 1:31-33). This covenant contains several important promises of God:

1. God would make a great name for David (2 Sam 7:9).

2. God would remove all external threats to the nation, i.e., give it "rest" (2 Sam 7:10-11).

3. One of David's offspring would build a temple (2 Sam 7:13).

4. God would build an eternal house (dynasty) through one of David's offspring (2 Sam 7:11, 13, 16; Luke 1:33).

5. One of David's offspring would rule an eternal kingdom (2 Sam 7:12-13, 16; Luke 1:33).

6. One of David's offspring would sit on an eternal throne (2 Sam 7:12-13, 16; Luke 1:32).

In a prayer to God, David reiterated the eternality of the promise "O Lord God, the word that Thou hast spoken concerning Thy servant and his house, confirm it forever...may it please Thee to bless the house of Thy servant, that it may continue forever before Thee...may the house of Thy servant be blessed forever" (2 Sam 7:25, 29).

The kingship in Israel approached its ideal in David but then fell short of its ultimate goal, the rule of righteousness. But the failure of David, then Solomon, and then the rest of the kings of Judah, did not abrogate or annul the covenant God had made with David. In Psalm 89, God bound himself to his promise concerning David and his descendants.

I have made a covenant with My chosen; I have sworn to David My servant, I will establish your seed forever and build up your throne to all generations (Ps 89:3-4).

The fact that God will grant the Messiah the power to "set his hand on the sea and his right hand on the rivers" indicates that an earthly dominion is meant.

"I shall also set his hand on the sea and his right hand on the rivers. He will cry to Me, 'You are my Father, My God, and the rock of my salvation.' I also shall make him *My* first born, the highest of the kings of the earth. My lovingkindness I will keep for him forever, and My covenant shall be confirmed to him. So I will establish his descendants forever and his throne as the days of heaven" (Ps 89:25-29).

"My covenant I will not violate, nor will I alter the utterance of My lips. Once I have sworn by My holiness; I will not lie to David. His descendants shall endure forever and his throne as the sun before Me. It shall be established forever like the moon, and the witness in the sky is faithful" (Ps 89:34-37).

By way of summary, the Davidic Covenant assured Israel that they would have a king from the line of David ruling a kingdom forever. This promise was never fully fulfilled in Old Testament history. Though Christ was identified as the rightful king, He was rejected by the Jews and crucified by the Romans at the behest of the Jewish leadership. Yet, after the Messiah's resurrection and ascension, Peter reveals that according to God's plan Jesus must remain in heaven until, "*the* period of restoration of all things about which God spoke by the mouth of His holy prophets from ancient time" is fulfilled (Acts 3:21). When that time is fulfilled, the Messiah will return to occupy the throne of David forever.

The Davidic throne has always been located in Jerusalem and is not to be confused with the throne of His Father in heaven from which He rules today (Acts 7:55; Heb 1:3; 8:1; 12:2). In his Pentecost sermon, Peter notes that Jesus fulfilled Psalm 110:1 in His ascension to the Father's right hand, "For it was not David who ascended into heaven, but he himself says: 'The Lord said to my Lord, Sit at My right hand until I make your enemies a footstool for your feet.'" (Acts 2:34-35).

Psalm 110:1 refers to Messiah's ascension to his heavenly throne, "The LORD says to my Lord: 'Sit at My right hand until I make Your enemies a footstool for Your feet'." This means the Messiah was first to be exalted to the honor of heaven before God would establish his rule on the earth, "whom heaven must receive until *the* period of restoration of all things about which God spoke by the mouth of His holy prophets from ancient time" (Acts 3:21). When the time for restoration arrived, the Messiah would return to rule as the next verse in Psalm 110 indicates, "The LORD will stretch forth Your strong scepter from Zion, *saying*, 'Rule in the midst of Your enemies.'" (Ps 110:2). Ruling on the throne of David in Jerusalem will extend through the millennial period. Following this, the Messiah will continue His rule into the new heaven and earth (Rev 21–22).

FULFILLMENT OF THE NEW COVENANT

One objection to worship in a millennial temple that I discussed earlier, was that Jesus clearly taught that a time was coming when worship of God would not be limited to a certain temple. Rather, true worship would be in "spirit and truth" (John 4:24). Thus, the objection is made that returning to a temple and sacrificial system would be a regression into an archaic form of worship. Let me emphasize that worship during the millennial setting in the Jerusalem temple will be "in spirit and truth." The hearts of the Jews and the Gentiles who partake in this worship will have been transformed. The New Covenant in which God pours out his Spirit into their hearts will have been inaugurated so that this new worship will not be perfunctory, lifeless, or without deep significance (cf. Isa 44:3; 59:22; Jer 31:31-33; Ezek 36:26-27; 37:14; 39:29). In fact, it will even be an advancement over that which the believer experiences today in the church age; for in the millennium the believer will not only worship "in spirit and truth" and be indwelt by the Holy Spirit, he will also have the distinct privilege of seeing God's manifest glory on earth by sojourning to the temple in Jerusalem (Isa 2:2-3; 4:5-6; Ezek 36:26-27; Zech 2:5, 11). We do not have that privilege today.

The New Covenant about which Jeremiah prophesied will be in effect. In contrast to the old Mosaic Covenant, it will succeed because God will put his laws in their hearts (Jer 31:33). The New Covenant involves a work of grace in the heart of each individual.

Today the church partakes in the New Covenant through faith in the Messiah (Mark 14:22-25; Luke 22:20). But eventually Israel will enter it at the time of her repentance and conversion to Christ (Isa 60–66; Zech 12:10-13:1; Rom 11:25-27).

Ezekiel is especially prolific in pointing out God's miraculous work in the hearts of the Israelites in and through the New Covenant:

I will make a covenant of peace with them; it will be an everlasting covenant with them. And I will place them and multiply them, and will set My sanctuary in their midst forever (Ezek 37:26).[10]

Note also in the citation below that Israel will have the Spirit, and yet follow certain "statues, and...ordinances,"

> Moreover, I will give you a new heart and put a new spirit within you; and I will remove the heart of stone from your flesh and give you a heart of flesh. I will put My Spirit within you and cause you to walk in My statutes, and you will be careful to observe My ordinances (Ezek 36:26-27).

Regarding the inward working of the Spirit on all of Israel, Ezekiel goes on to say,

> "I will put My Spirit within you and you will come to life, and I will place you on your own land. Then you will know that I, the LORD, have spoken and done it," declares the LORD. (Ezek 37:14).

> "I will not hide My face from them any longer, for I will have poured out My Spirit on the house of Israel," declares the Lord God (Ezek 39:29).

---

10   See my earlier comments on the range of meaning for the term "forever" (*'olam*), on pages 140-141.

CHAPTER 13

RESTORATION OF THE EARTH

In the book of Revelation, near the end of the trumpet judgments, voices in heaven announce that Christ has seized the kingdoms of the earth (Rev 11:15). The elders in heaven declare that the time has arrived for God to "destroy those who destroy the earth" (Rev 11:18). Ostensibly, while much devastation on the earth has been caused by the hand of man, God's future direct judgment will bring utter devastation. Isaiah tells us, "Behold, the LORD lays the earth waste, devastates it, distorts its surface and scatters its inhabitants" (Isa 24:1).

The prophet Zephaniah adds,

> "I will completely remove all *things* from the face of the earth," declares the LORD. I will remove man and beast; I will remove the birds of the sky and the fish of the sea, and the ruins along with the wicked; and I will cut off man from the face of the earth," declares the LORD (Zeph 1:2-3).

Nahum appears to refer to the same general upheaval,

> Mountains quake because of Him and the hills dissolve; indeed the earth is upheaved by His presence, the world

and all the inhabitants in it. Who can stand before His indignation? Who can endure the burning of His anger? His wrath is poured out like fire and the rocks are broken up by Him (Nah 1:5-6).

These judgments, chronicled in Revelation 6–19, climax and come to an end with the Second Coming of Christ to earth, an event mentioned by many of the New Testament writers. Once Christ secures direct control of the earth and the remaining governments of the world, he will begin his millennial reign initiating a new world order. At that time Christ will begin to restore the ravaged earth. This restoration will include several transformations noted by the Scriptures.

GEOGRAPHICAL AND TOPOGRAPHICAL CHANGES

The Bible points to specific topographical changes that will take place in and around Jerusalem at Christ's Second Coming,

> In that day His feet will stand on the Mount of Olives, which is in front of Jerusalem on the east; and the Mount of Olives will be split in its middle from east to west by a very large valley, so that half of the mountain will move toward the north and the other half toward the south (Zech 14:4).

In conjunction with his return or shortly thereafter, Jerusalem and the temple mount will be raised up to a higher physical location than it now occupies,

> Now it will come about that in the last days the mountain of the house of the LORD will be established as the chief of the mountains and will be raised above the hills; and all the nations will stream to it. And many peoples will come and say, "Come, let us go up to the mountain of the LORD" (Isa 2:2).

The prophet Micah restates the same prophecy (Mic 4:1-3). Some expositors have proposed that both Isaiah and Micah were expressing spiritual realities about Jerusalem rather than giving literal physical descriptions. But Ezekiel in his vision of the millennial temple confirms this point. He says that God brought him to Jerusalem and set him, "on a very high mountain, and on it to the south *there was* a structure like a city" (Ezek 40:2). That city would be Jerusalem and it has been raised up geographically according to the prophet's vision. Around Jerusalem the geography of the land will also be changed,

> All the land will be changed into a plain from Geba to Rimmon south of Jerusalem; but Jerusalem will rise and remain on its site from Benjamin's Gate as far as the place of the First Gate to the Corner Gate, and from the Tower of Hananel to the king's wine presses (Zech 14:10).

Geba was located six miles north of Jerusalem on the northern border of Judah but within the tribe of Benjamin (Josh 21:17; 1 Sam13:3; 2 Kgs 23:8). Rimmon lies thirty miles south of Jerusalem in the far south of Judah (Josh 15:32; Job 15:32). So, Zechariah is referring to an extensive geographical transformation of the area cited.

In Old Testament times Jerusalem was surrounded by mountains or hills as it is today (Ps 121:1; 125:2). So, Zechariah is saying the whole central part of Israel will become a plain while Jerusalem will be raised up. Literally the phrase reads, "all around the land will be like the Arabah." The Arabah is the "plain" (or valley) which extends from Mount Hermon in the north (on the Lebanon-Syrian border) to the Dead Sea in the south. Whatever the exact boundary of this plain will be, it appears to be a change affecting much the land of Israel so that Jerusalem will be exalted and raised up as the capital city of Israel.

At the end of the millennial period, when the last rebellion takes place, the invading armies approach Jerusalem possibly by way of this plain, "And they came up on the broad plain of the earth and surrounded the camp of the saints" (Rev 20:9). This is significant since today Jerusalem is surrounded by hills not by plains.

Ezekiel refers to a time of future enhanced blessing when a new river will flow from the temple eastward and southward into the Dead Sea. The prophet describes an Eden-like state, "Living waters will flow out from Jerusalem, half of them towards the eastern sea and half of them towards the western sea," and "everything will live where the river goes" (14:8-9). The psalmist may be referring to this river when he writes, "There is a river whose streams make glad the city of God" (Ps 46:4). These waters will teem with fish-life and transform the salt water of the Dead Sea into fresh water. On its banks, trees will grow providing fruit monthly, and their leaves will provide healing properties. All this envisions a glorious day yet to come (Ezek 47:1-12).

Other than these limited descriptions, we do not know to what degree other regions of the earth will be changed, but if we consider the judgments cited by Old Testament prophets and confirmed by the book of Revelation, it seems that the devastations will be considerable. Jesus compared the time of these judgments to the great Noahic flood in which much of the surface of the world was ravaged (Luke 17:26-27; 2 Pet 3:6-7). Isaiah prophesied of a future widespread destruction, "Behold, the LORD lays the earth waste, devastates it, distorts its surface and scatters its inhabitants" (Isa 24:1).

This implies that at the conclusion of these judgments world geography and climate will have been negatively affected. Yet Christ assures us that the world will not be completely destroyed as many fear, but it would have been if the Lord had not returned when he does, "Unless those days had been cut short, no life would have been saved; but for the sake of the elect those days will be cut short" (Matt 24:22). God will save the world from total destruction and humankind from annihilation. Ezekiel assures us that Christ will reverse the effects of his judgments, "The cities will be inhabited and the waste places will be rebuilt" (Ezek 36:10). After his Second Advent, Christ will implement climatic and ecological changes that return the earth to a state of blessing.

CLIMATIC & ECOLOGICAL CHANGES

David may be describing this time of blessing and fertility in nature in Psalm 65,

> They who dwell in the ends *of the earth* stand in awe of Your signs; You make the dawn and the sunset shout for joy. You visit the earth and cause it to overflow; You greatly enrich it; the stream of God is full of water; You prepare their grain, for thus You prepare the earth. You water its furrows abundantly, You settle its ridges, You soften it with showers, You bless its growth. You have crowned the year with Your bounty, and Your paths drip *with* fatness. The pastures of the wilderness drip, and the hills gird themselves with rejoicing. The meadows are clothed with flocks and the valleys are covered with grain; they shout for joy, yes, they sing (Ps 65:8-13).

Though in a general sense we may attribute such blessings to God, even in our own times, but the fact that here it is worldwide "the ends *of the earth*" makes one suspect that David was projecting the future blessing of Christ's millennial reign. Surely all the earth has not yet sung to God in joy over its bounty as verse 13 intimates. Isaiah refers to favorable climatic changes in which the wilderness and desert will be transformed,

> The wilderness and the desert will be glad, and the Arabah will rejoice and blossom; like the crocus it will blossom profusely...For waters will break forth in the wilder-

ness and streams in the Arabah…The scorched land will become a pool and the thirsty ground springs of water (Isa 35:1-2, 6-7).

In addition, trees and plants will flourish,

I will open rivers on the bare heights and springs in the midst of the valleys; I will make the wilderness a pool of water and the dry land fountains of water. I will put the cedar in the wilderness, the acacia and the myrtle and the olive tree; I will place the juniper in the desert together with the box tree and the cypress, that they may see and recognize, and consider and gain insight as well, that the hand of the LORD has done this, and the Holy One of Israel has created it (Isa 41:18-20).

Instead of the thorn bush the cypress will come up, and instead of the nettle the myrtle will come up, and it will be a memorial to the LORD, for an everlasting sign which will not be cut off (Isa 55:13).

In the context of Jews returning to the promised land, probably after the Second Coming, Isaiah says, "They will not hunger or thirst, nor will the scorching heat or sun strike them down; for He who has compassion on them will lead them and will guide them to springs of water" (Isa 49:10).

The psalmist also speaks prophetically when he looks forward to a day of more favorable climates, "The LORD is your keeper; the LORD is your shade on your right hand. The sun will not smite you by day, nor the moon by night" (Ps 121:5-6).

The Apostle John confirms this in promising removal of famines and drought,

They will hunger no longer, nor thirst anymore; nor will the sun beat down on them, nor any heat (Rev 7:16)

The psalmist looks forward to time when crops will be blessed, "May there be abundance of grain in the land; on the tops of the mountains may it wave; may its fruit be like Lebanon; and may people blossom in the cities like the grass of the field!" (Ps 72:16).

God pictures himself as sowing grain, "And in that day I will answer, declares the LORD, I will answer the heavens, and they shall answer the earth, and the earth shall answer the grain, the wine, and the oil, and they shall answer Jezreel [Jezreel means God will sow], and I will sow her for myself in the land" (Hos 2:21-23). The only exception will be for any nation that rebels against God's millennial rule for which the Lord will withhold rain as a judgment (Zech 14:16-19).

> Then it will come about that any who are left of all the nations that went against Jerusalem will go up from year to year to worship the King, the LORD of hosts, and to celebrate the Feast of Booths. And it will be that whichever of the families of the earth does not go up to Jerusalem to worship the King, the LORD of hosts, there will be no rain on them. If the family of Egypt does not go up or enter, then no *rain will fall* on them; it will be the plague with which the LORD smites the nations who do not go up to celebrate the Feast of Booths. This will be the punishment of Egypt, and the punishment of all the nations who do not go up to celebrate the Feast of Booths.

INCREASED LIFESPANS, REMOVAL OF CALAMITIES AND SICKNESS

After the fall of man, death entered the human race (Gen 2:15; Rom 5:12). During the primeval days of the earth, the age span of the antediluvian civilization was limited to 900 plus years. After the flood, age spans began to drop precipitously until they tapered off to 70 or 80 years on average, "The years of our life are seventy, or even by reason of strength eighty; yet their span is but toil and trouble; they are soon gone, and we fly away" (Ps 90:10).

In Isaiah 65:20 the prophet describes a time when people will again enjoy longer lifespans and premature death will be eliminated.

> No longer will there be in it an infant *who lives but a few* days, or an old man who does not live out his days; for the youth will die at the age of one hundred and the one who does not reach the age of one hundred will be *thought* accursed (Isa 65:20).

Obviously, Isaiah is not talking about the eternal state in this verse (though he does mention it previously in verses 17-19) because he refers here to old age, death and the possibility of being accursed.[11] So, the curse and death are still in effect, but lifespans have increased so much so that if a person dies at 100 years old, people will consider him to have been cursed by God. In other words, living such a short life span—just 100 years—will be very unusual.

I cited a few of the following verses earlier in other contexts but repeat them here to shed light specifically on lifespans in the millennium.

> They will build houses and inhabit *them*; they will also plant vineyards and eat their fruit. They will not build and another inhabit, they will not plant and another eat; for as the lifetime of a tree, *so will be* the days of My people, and My chosen ones will wear out the work of their hands. They will not labor in vain, or bear *children* for calamity; for they are the offspring of those blessed by the LORD,

---

11   Ezekiel, in describing the ministry of the priests in the millennial temple, prohibits them from defiling themselves by coming near a dead person, except for an immediate family member. This is another indication that sin and death is still in effect, though greatly ameliorated, during the millennial era (Ezek 44:25).

and their descendants with them. It will also come to pass that before they call, I will answer; and while they are still speaking, I will hear (Isa 65:22-24).

Several descriptions in the above paragraph indicate that the prophet is referring to the millennial condition not the eternal state. He says, "They will build houses and inhabit them." By way of contrast, in the eternal state we will dwell in the Father's house, the New Jerusalem (cf. John 14:1-3; Rev 21:9-14). In the millennial setting, God's people will plant vineyards. This could be possible in the eternal state but fits better with the building of houses, and thus describing a future condition on this earth. Comparing lifespans to that of a tree means they will live longer, but even a tree eventually dies, but not so for the person who has entered the new heaven and earth.

The prophet Zechariah also makes clear that men and women will age in the millennium,

> Thus says the LORD, "I will return to Zion and will dwell in the midst of Jerusalem. Then Jerusalem will be called the City of Truth, and the mountain of the LORD of hosts *will be called* the Holy Mountain." Thus says the LORD of hosts, "Old men and old women will again sit in the streets of Jerusalem, each man with his staff in his hand because of age. And the streets of the city will be filled with boys and girls playing in its streets" (Zech 8:3-5).

If we assume in the new heaven and earth we will not grow old, then the above passage by Zechariah could hardly be a referring to the eternal state, since he refers to old men and old women walking with the help of a staff in their hands. More likely he is describing the millennial state after the return of Christ when he will be present in Jerusalem in a unique way.

The Apostle Paul maintains that "The last enemy to be destroyed is death" (1 Cor 15:26). Physical death will not be eradicated until the onset of the new heaven and earth. Isaiah also promised that God's people will not be taken advantage of or face calamity. This would not be necessary to say if no enemies and no accidents or death existed as will be the case in eternity (Rev 21:4). Also, the fact that people are still laboring and giving birth to children negates the possibility that these verses describe the new heaven and earth, for Jesus said regarding the eternal state, "For when they rise from the dead, they neither marry nor are given in marriage, but are like angels in heaven" (Mark 12:25). Ezekiel also refers to the Israelites dividing up the land among themselves and bearing children during the millennial age (Ezek 47:21-22). Neither will take place in the new heaven and earth. Finally, the promise in Isaiah 65:24 is that God will answer immediately when someone calls out to him. This implies that it is a call for help, which all of us know does not automatically or immediately happen when we pray today. In the eternal state there will be no need to call for rescue. Most likely this promise of a quick answer to prayer by God is one of the benefits and blessings to come about with the introduction of the millennial era.

In addition, sickness, particularly ailments brought on because of iniquities will be greatly reduced, "And no inhabitant will say, 'I am sick'; the people who dwell there will be forgiven their iniquity" (cf. Isa 33:24; 1 Cor 11:30; Jas 5:13-15). By way of contrast, there will be no sin or sickness at all in the new heaven and earth (Rev 21:4, 27; 22:3).

The blind, lame, mute, deaf, and presumably other debilitating sicknesses, shall be healed, "Then the eyes of the blind shall be opened, and the ears of the deaf unstopped; then shall the lame man leap like a deer, and the tongue of the mute sing for joy" (Isa 35:5-6). The Messiah performed healings like these at

166

his First Advent to prove his claims and signal the presence of his kingdom, but they will be proliferated world-wide at his Second Avent (Matt 11:5).

The desire for God to return the earth to state of physical blessing, and the confidence that he will do so is expressed by the psalmist,

> Let our sons in their youth be as grown-up plants, and our daughters as corner pillars fashioned as for a palace; Let our garners be full, furnishing every kind of produce, *and* our flocks bring forth thousands and ten thousands in our fields; let our cattle bear without mishap and without loss, *let there be* no outcry in our streets! How blessed are the people who are so situated; how blessed are the people whose God is the LORD! (Ps 144:12-15).

HARMONY IN THE ANIMAL KINGDOM AND WITH MANKIND

One other phenomenal reality that will characterize the millennial kingdom on earth is a new harmony within the animal kingdom among the species and in their interaction with humans. When God created man, He did so with the mandate to rule over the animal world, "Be fruitful and multiply, and fill the earth, and subdue it; and rule over the fish of the sea and over the birds of the sky and over every living thing that moves on the earth." With the entrance of sin into the world, man lost the effectiveness of that dominion to a great degree (Gen 1:28; 3:1-6). One result was the disturbance in the harmony between the animal world and man.

In preparation for the Flood, God told Noah that two of every kind of animal "will come to you" (Gen 6:20). But after the Flood, God placed a fear of man within animals, bringing about a greater alienation between the animal kingdom and mankind, resulting in or exacerbating the ferocious, aggressive, and fearful behavior of some of the species (Gen 9:2). This was one of the results of sin entering into the world. Yet, this state of fear and/or aggression among the animals will apparently be removed by God in the millennial era. Hosea notes that God will directly bring about this change, "In that day I will also make a covenant for them with the beasts of the field, the birds of the sky and the creeping things of the ground" (Hos 2:18). But it is Isaiah who is most descriptive of this new situation,

> And the wolf will dwell with the lamb, and the leopard will lie down with the young goat, and the calf and the young lion and the fatling together; and a little boy will lead them. Also the cow and the bear will graze, their young will lie down together, and the lion will eat straw like the ox. The nursing child will play by the hole of the cobra, and the weaned child will put his hand on the viper's den. They will not hurt or destroy in all My holy mountain, for the earth will be full of the knowledge of the LORD as the waters cover the sea (Isa 11:6-9).

Not only does Isaiah see harmony in the animal kingdom but also between the animals and mankind. Later the prophet again announces this new and amazing condition that God will bring about,

> "The wolf and the lamb will graze together, and the lion will eat straw like the ox; and dust will be the serpent's food. They will do no evil or harm in all My holy mountain," says the LORD (Isa 65:25).

It is perhaps this change that will allow man to finally realize and successfully fulfill the creation mandate of ruling over the animal kingdom.

THE CREATION MANDATE FULFILLED

The Bible begins with God issuing a creation mandate to Adam and Eve. They were to multiply, fill the earth and rule over the animal kingdom. Since they were to procreate, it is clear that the whole human race was to take part in fulfilling the mandate. This purpose was interrupted and greatly hindered by the entrance of sin into creation. Rather than giving up on his purpose or destroying the creation and beginning a new one, God determines to redeem and restore the old creation in an unfolding step by step plan that only becomes clear to us through his progressive revelation.

The plan began with the announcement of it in Genesis 3:15 whereby God would bring into the world One who would crush and defeat Satan (Rom 16:20; Heb 2:14). Further revelation clarifies that he elected a family line and nation through which he would bring his plan of restoration to pass. Through the Abrahamic family the king who would one day rule the world would come (Gen 17:8; 2 Sam 7:14-16; Isa 9:4-6; Luke 1:30-31; Rev 11:15). This king would defeat the works of the devil (Heb 2:14-15) and bring many sons [and daughters] to glory through their spiritual salvation and physical resurrection. By co-ruling with him, he would lead the human race to fulfill the original creation mandate of having dominion over the earth (Gen 1:28; Heb 2:5-10).

We may assume that in the millennial era man will continue to carry out the mandate to multiply and fill the earth, subdue the creation, and rule over the whole earth, including the animal kingdom. The resurrected saints will not take part in procreation, but those Jews and Gentiles who survive the Day of the Lord and enter into the millennial kingdom in their earthly bodies will. The resurrected saints will be co-rulers with Christ (2 Tim 2:12; Rev 5:10; 11:15; 20:6). Those entering the millennium in their earthly bodies will be participants of the kingdom. In this way, God will bring to fruition his original creation mandate.

169

Some rightly argue that the idealization or perfection of God's creation will not be reached until the eternal state. Yet in several ways the eternal state described in Revelation 21–22 is not the fulfillment of the original creation mandate but goes well beyond it.

For example, in the original mandate man and wife were to procreate to fill the earth. In eternity Jesus clarifies that marriage will not continue as it did in the first creation (Mark 12:25). Thus, procreation will not take place. That part of the mandate would need to be completed before we enter eternity. By way of contrast, in the millennium marriage and pro-creation will continue among those who enter the kingdom so that mankind can fill the whole earth.

Also, in the original creation mandate, mankind was tasked with subduing the earth, in the sense of bringing it under his care and control. In the millennium with Christ ruling, mankind will finally be able to subdue the earth. By way of contrast, the new creation will not need to be subdued or brought under control.

In the original mandate, God charged man to rule over the fish of the sea, birds of the air, and all the creatures on the earth. Because of man's increased sin before the flood (Gen 6:5-8) and God instilling in his creatures the fear of man after the flood (Gen 9:2), man has never been able to completely fulfill this task. Yet, in the millennial reign, God promises to remove the natural enmity between the animal kingdom and humanity as we saw in the passages from Isaiah above (Isa 11:6-9; 65:25).

Some expositors have proposed that the original creation mandate will not be fulfilled in a millennium but in the new heaven and earth. They have suggested that even animals may be resurrected or created for the new creation. However, the Scripture is noticeably silent on the resurrection and/or creation of such creatures for the eternal state. Though such a scenario is possible, it remains an argument from silence.

There are reasons for maintaining that the millennium will be a consummation of the creation mandate. For example, in the original mandate Moses writes,

> God blessed them; and God said to them, "Be fruitful and multiply, and fill the earth, and subdue it; and rule over the fish of the sea and over the birds of the sky and over every living thing that moves on the earth."

But the Apostle John states that there will be no sea in the new heaven and earth, "Then I saw a new heaven and a new earth; for the first heaven and the first earth passed away, and there is no longer *any* sea." If we are interpreting the apostle correctly, then there would be no "fish of sea" to rule over in the new heaven and earth, thus the original creation mandate would not apply. But in the millennial state, as mentioned, the Messiah will rule "from sea to sea" (Ps 72:8; Zech 9:10). Thus, there would be creatures of the sea to subdue and rule over. In the millennial state we have seen that the beasts of the field will live harmony with other animals and with mankind, but we have no revelation indicating that these beasts will occupy the eternal state.

Conclusion

The Vindication of Messiah on Earth

By way of summary, I have suggested that an Edenic-like state will be restored to the earth during the millennium. One major difference is that in Eden, before Satan's intrusion into the garden, Adam and Eve lived not only in a perfect environment, but they were also untainted by sin. In the millennial age, the condition of the earth and mankind will be greatly improved but not yet perfected. Those who enter the kingdom in their natural bodies, that is those who are alive on the earth after Christ's return, will be redeemed but not yet perfected (all rebels living at the time of the Second Coming will have been judged with physical death). The offspring of those entering the kingdom in their earthly bodies will inherit the Adamic nature from their parents and need to experience redemption and forgiveness for their own sin. By way of contrast, the saints of all the ages who have been resurrected to participate in Christ's rule will be perfected and intermingle with the people of the earth who will be their natural bodies, much like Christ did after his resurrection.

I have tried to show that the Scriptures abundantly testify to the rule of the Messiah on the (old) earth. His reign will serve as a wonderful climax to human history. It will be an era in God's plan that brings him unparalleled glory. From a pragmatic standpoint, it will provide the setting on earth in which Jesus, having brought many sons and daughters to glory, will lead mankind in fulfilling its original creation mandate. Thus, Satan will not have decisively thwarted God's plan or successfully usurped His rule. In addition, it will be a period when many of the ancient promises made by God to His people (primarily the patriarchs, Israel, and the church), will be realized. God will demonstrate His unfailing faithfulness in bringing the promises contained in the Abrahamic, Davidic, and New Covenants to fulfillment. Finally, it will be a time in human history when God will vindicate His Messiah on earth before men and angels.

This viewpoint does not deny that God's ultimate goal will find it fulfillment in the new heaven and earth. We see this by simply comparing and contrasting the beginning of the Bible with the end. It begins with the creation of the heavens and the earth and ends with the creation of a new heaven and new earth (cf. Gen 1:1; Rev 21:1). It began with man's fellowship with God being severed and ends with that fellowship restored and perfected (cf. Gen 3:8; Rev 21:3). At the beginning marriage was instituted by God but in the new creation there will be no marriage (cf. Gen 2:24; Matt 12:23-24). In the first creation the sun, moon, and stars served as the light but in the new creation the Lamb is the eternal light (Gen 1:14-16; Rev 21:23). The Bible begins in a garden but ends in an eternal city (Gen 2; Rev 21–22). In the beginning there was the potential for good or evil, life or death; but in the end, there will be no possibility of evil and no death (cf. Gen 2:9-17; 3:1-8; Rev 21:4, 8). Some of God's ultimate purposes will find their final fulfillment in the new heaven and earth, but many of God's historical purposes will reach their goal before that final state in the millennium.

When we look at what falls between the beginning and the end, the so-called book ends of the Bible (the creation and the new creation), it becomes clear, that except for a few scattered statements and the last two chapters, very little is said about the eternal state. In fact, only the last two chapters give a detailed account of it. By way of contrast, the overwhelming preponderance of biblical revelation focuses on the historical movement, incrementally step by step, from the fall of man to the redemption procured by the Messiah, and then climatically to his reign on this earth. This climatic reign should not be ignored or belittled.

From the standpoint of the church, redemption, and the new heaven and earth may seem most important to us. However, from the perspective of God as provided through the Biblical Corpus of divine revelation, the vindication of the Messiah on the earth is the climactic event in biblical history, and eternity serves as the final resolution to it. Thus, the chronological movement of the Bible, from Genesis 3 to Revelation 20 reveals the historical development and theological unfolding of God's purpose to re-establish his Messiah's rule over the earth with the redeemed. It starts with God's rule being interrupted in Genesis 3, but ends with his rule being reestablished in Revelation 20.

I began this book by stating that the Bible is arguably the most read book in the world today and in human history. According to *Guinness World Records*, it is the best-selling book of all time. But then I posed the question, what makes this book so popular? What is it all about? What is the general over-all subject matter of the Bible? It is about many things, but what it is mainly about? Redemption? Yes, but it's more than that. Although the opening two chapters and final two chapters serve as the bookends to this epic drama, I have argued that between these bookends lies the massive revelation of the Bible, in which the writers of Scripture focus on the major stages and progressive unfolding of God's purpose of recovering mankind from the fall, regaining the earth, and establishing Messiah's rule over it.

In the original creation Satan was free to intrude and roam (Gen 3:1-6; Job 1-2), but at the end he will be first imprisoned for a thousand years and then consigned to the lake of fire for ever and ever (Rev 20:1-10). At the beginning of human history God's rule was rejected, but at the end of human history—even before entering the eternal state—God's Messiah shall rule from sea to sea.

In each era or administration of salvation history, God advances what He is doing for man redemptively. He moves his plan forward chronologically until he installs His King on Mount

Zion. History is moving inexorably toward this goal: Messiah will be vindicated; the Son shall reign on the earth.

> "But as for Me, I have installed My King upon Zion, My holy mountain. I will surely tell of the decree of the LORD: He said to Me, 'You are My Son, today I have begotten You. Ask of Me, and I will surely give the nations as Your inheritance, and the *very* ends of the earth as Your possession. You shall break them with a rod of iron, You shall shatter them like earthenware'" (Ps 2:6-9).

Appendix

Synopsis of the plan for a kingdom on earth: A king and a kingdom were prophesied (2 Sam 7:12-16; Ps 72; 89:3-4; Isa 9:6-7). The king arrived (Matt 1:1, 17; Luke 1:31-33). He offered his kingdom (Matt 4:17). He and his kingdom were rejected. The Messiah was crucified and resurrected. In light of the rejection, the kingdom offer was withdrawn (Matt 21:43). New revelation about the kingdom in the present age was given (Matt 13). The cancellation of the kingdom will last until the nation repents (Matt 23:39). The Messiah and his kingdom will come in the future (Matt 16:28-17:8; 24:30; Rev 19:11-16). The Messiah will reign on the earth in the kingdom (Rev 20:1-6).

TRACING THE KINGDOM ON EARTH CONCEPT THROUGH THE OT & NT

1. They lost their ability to rule adequately at the fall (Gen 3:1-24).

2. God works in a progressive plan (throughout the Bible) to restore man's rule under his rule, through the Messiah, over the earth (Gen 3:15).

3. He chooses the Abrahamic family to create a nation through which he will bring the Messiah (Gen 12–Exod 1).

4. He gives them a constitution (covenant) and a land that will become the center of the Messiah's realm (Exod 19–24; Josh 1–18).

5. God's glory takes up residency among his people first in the tabernacle (Exod 40:34-38) and later in the temple (1 Kgs 8:10-13).

6.   He inaugurates a monarchy (1 Sam 1–12; 16) and promises a messianic ruler and an ideal kingdom (2 Sam 7:12-16; Ps 72; 89:3-4; Isa 9:6-7).

7.   The nation fails to obey God and is severally disciplined in the Assyrian and Babylonian captivities (2 Kgs 17; 24–25).

8.   The end of the Davidic monarchy in Judah and the departure of the glory of God from the temple signaled the temporary termination of the Davidic dynasty (Ezek 8:3-4; 9:3; 10:3-4, 18-19; 11:22-23).

9.   The nation returns to the land, but the theocracy and kingdom are not reinstituted (Ezra, Nehemiah, Malachi). The glory does not return, and a king is not appointed.

10. Israel waits some 400 years for its Davidic king (between the Testaments).

11. The Messiah arrives as the promised King offering the reestablishment of the Davidic kingdom (Matt 1–4; Lk 1:32-33).

12. He teaches the subjects of his kingdom about his kingdom (Matt 5–7; John 3).

13. His miracles demonstrate he is the Messiah and has the power to bring in his kingdom (Matt 8–9).

14. But he is rejected as the Messiah by Israel (Matt 12–27).

15. He gives new truth about his kingdom in light of his rejection (Matt 13).

16. The kingdom offer (i.e. the Messiah's immediate earthly rule) is temporarily withdrawn (Matt 21:43) yet promised to come in power in the future (Matt 24:30).

17. The Messiah dies for the nation and the whole world (Isa 53; Matt 26–28).

18. God begins to build his church of Jews and Gentiles who will co-rule in the coming kingdom (Acts 2–Rev 3).

19. Israel is driven out of the land by the Romans in AD 70 (and returns to the land gaining statehood in 1948).

20. Still future: God judges Israel and the nations (Ezek 20; Isa 24–27; Matt 24; Rev 4–19).

21. The Messiah returns to establish his millennial rule upon the earth (Zech 14:3-4; Matt 24:30; Rev 19-20).

22. The millennial kingdom merges into the eternal kingdom (1 Cor 15:24-28; Rev 21–22).

ALSO AVAILABLE FROM LAMPION HOUSE PUBLISHING

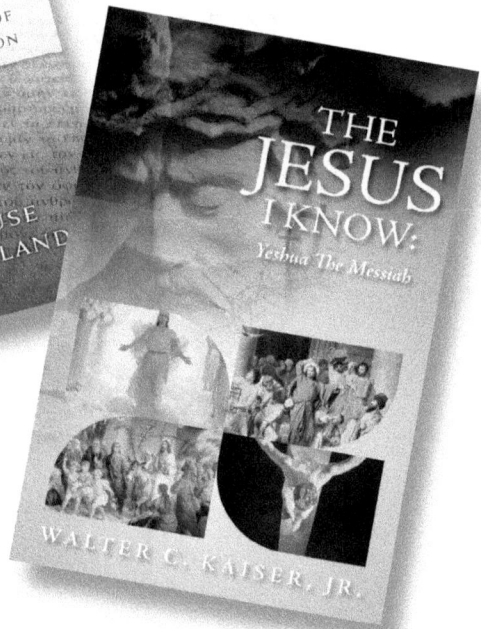

LOOK FOR THESE AND OTHER GREAT TITLES AT:

LAMPIONHOUSEPUBLISHING.COM

www.ingramcontent.com/pod-product-compliance
Lightning Source LLC
Chambersburg PA
CBHW051421090426
42737CB00014B/2767